The
Promise
To
Love

The Promise To Love

A SCRIPTURAL VIEW OF MARRIAGE

WILFRID J. HARRINGTON, O.P.

alba house DIVISION OF THE SOCIETY OF ST. PAUL   STATEN ISLAND, N.Y. 10314

Nihil Obstat:

    John A. Goodwine, J.C.D.

    Censor Librorum

Imprimatur:

    ✝ Terence J. Cooke, D.D., V.G.

    New York, N.Y., October 18, 1967

Library of Congress Catalog Card Number: 68-15381

For

Don and Laura Reilly

KEY TO BIBLICAL WRITINGS CITED

Gen	Genesis	Hos	Hosea
Ex	Exodus	Mal	Malachi
Lev	Leviticus	2 Mac	2 Maccabees
Dt	Deuteronomy	Mt	Matthew
Jg	Judges	Mk	Mark
Ruth	Ruth	Lk	Luke
1 Sam	1 Samuel	Jn	John
2 Sam	2 Samuel	Acts	Acts of the Apostles
2 Kg	2 Kings	Rom	Romans
1 Chr	1 Chronicles	1 Cor	1 Corinthians
Ez	Ezra	2 Cor	2 Corinthians
Neh	Nehemiah	Gal	Galatians
Tob	Tobit	Eph	Ephesians
Ps	Psalm	Phil	Philippians
Prov	Proverbs	Col	Colossians
Qoh	Qohelet (Ecclesiastes)	1 Thes	1 Thessalonians
Song	Song of Songs	2 Thes	2 Thessalonians
Wis	Wisdom	1 Tim	1 Timothy
Sir	Sirach (Ecclesiasticus)	Tit	Titus
Is	Isaiah	Heb	Hebrews
Jer	Jeremiah	Jas	James
Ezek	Ezekiel	1 Pet	1 Peter
		Apoc	Apocalypse

Contents

Preface

It is commonplace that, until recent years, there was scant appreciation, not to say lack of realization, of the true place of the laity in the Church. This had unhappy results in our understanding of marriage. But whether or not the overall outlook was the real cause it is a fact that our theology of marriage was defective. In theological manuals, at this point, the moral theologian ceded to the canonist and the treatment of a sacrament became an outline of Catholic legislation on marriage. This was true of the first part, at least, of the tract; the rest was a depressing catalogue of the "sins of married people." A glance at a typical manual will bear us out.

The call for a renewal of moral theology, an insistent call which modern theologians are meeting, sounds most poignantly just here. Our young men and women, married or contemplating marriage, are candidly dissatisfied with a presentation of marriage that sees only its legal and biological aspects. Instinctively they feel that there is more to it than this. Human beings are not only flesh and blood and man does not live by law alone. There must be a place for love in this most intimate of human relations; there must be challenge and scope for the full expression of human personality. And so theologians have taken another look at marriage. What they have discovered is reflected in the documents of the Second Vatican Council, especially in the Constitution on *The Church in the Modern World*.

The Council Fathers have given us a Christian understanding of marriage which stresses the basic value of conjugal love. No longer can it be maintained that the procreation and education of children are the only meaningful ends of marriage, for marriage is first and foremost a personal relationship. It is pointed out that the Scriptures "urge the bethrothed and the married to nourish and develop their wedlock by pure conjugal love and undivided affection." Since conjugal love involves the good of the whole person, the essential goodness of sexual love and its important place in marriage are candidly avowed. In short, we have turned away from a negative and inadequate view of marriage to a positive and rewarding approach. Here, as in the whole field of theological renewal, theologians have gone back to the source, to the Word of God. And that is what we shall do in this book. We may be surprised (and shall certainly be encouraged) by what we find.

II

The biblical view of marriage follows from the biblical understanding of man.

> What is man that you are mindful of him,
>   the son of man, that you care for him?
> You have made him little less than a god,
>   crowning him with glory and splendor
>   (Ps 8:5ff).

So speaks the psalmist—surely a hopeless optimist! Yet, when we view this passage against its Old Testament background we realize that it is profoundly true. The biblical writers are quite well aware that man is not a paragon of perfection, but they also know that God created man in his own image and they are sure that God has not abandoned him. They believe that, even yet, he is the pride of God's creation.

It is good for us to consider this. If we are to live an integral Christian life it is not enough for us to be conscious of our misery, and there is little to be gained by dwelling on shortcomings and sin unless positive values are stressed much more. It is not sufficient merely to have pointed out to us what we ought to do; what we need above all else is an ideal, something to strive after, something to live by.

This has particular relevance in the sphere of married life. We have not heard enough about the dignity of that state. It has not been brought home to us with sufficient emphasis that the salvation of the married is to be sought and won within this way of life: as husbands and wives, as fathers and mothers. And so, many do not come to know the marvel of God's plan, simply because they lack the pointer that could tell them where they might learn of it. If we are to be true, not only to the letter but to the very spirit of the Second Vatican Council we should strive without delay to make good this lack.

This little work is meant to be such a signpost. It is patently not a full treatment of the Bible's teaching on marriage, but it does, I feel, give some idea of the Creator's view of marriage. In the beginning he made mankind male and female and blessed their union. When they fell he did not abandon them but gave them the grace to rise. And in his Scriptures God set a standard that was progressively raised to match the progress of revelation: monogamous marriage, the marriage-image of Yahweh and Israel, the marriage-type of Christ and his Church.

The Bible is never merely negative; surely because

God knows us so much better than we know our-selves. This is why it is the one unfailing source of a sound and balanced spirituality, why it shows us, very clearly, the meaning and purpose of life. It is unthink-able that it should have no teaching on a matter so fundamentally human as marriage. And we do in-deed find a message here: Like man himself, marriage has come from God; like man, it has been redeemed by the Son of God. Husbands and wives can find, within marriage, salvation and sanctity.

W. J. H.

PART ONE

Chapter One
The Prototype of Marriage

Though it really should not surprise us, it is at least thought-provoking that the essential doctrine on marriage is presented in the opening chapters of the Bible. The subject comes up quite naturally because the two accounts of creation in Genesis chapters 1 and 2, though differing in many respects, agree in laying notable emphasis on the formation of man. They make the point, each in its own distinctive way, that this creature is unlike all others, that he is made in God's image. But they also insist—just as emphatically—that the difference of sex was intended by God in view of marriage, that it is an essential part of the divine plan for mankind. If we are to grasp this teaching we shall need to know something about the literary construction and forms of these first chapters of Genesis.[1]

---

1. See W. J. Harrington, **Record of Revelation: The Old Testament** (Chicago: The Priory Press, 1965), pp. 101-142.

Four Traditions

It is now accepted that the Pentateuch (the first five books of the Bible, Genesis to Deuteronomy) in the main, is a combination of four traditions. The earliest of these is called 'Yahwistic' because it employs the name Yahweh—the special name for God in the Old Testament—right from the creation narrative. This tradition is undoubtedly of Judean origin and received its final form in the tenth century, during the peaceful reign of Solomon. The style of the Yahwist is distinctive. He loves concrete and striking expressions and excels in describing character. He writes with liveliness, clarity, and polish and is able to sketch a scene with a few bold strokes. Though a profound theologian, he wears his theological proficiency so lightly that his purpose can be misunderstood. Thus, in images, with apparent naiveté, he gives a profound answer to the grave problems which are raised by the presence of evil in the good world made by God. He asks, for instance, why death, the pains of woman, the sweat of man (Gen 3)? The moral development (or rather retrogression) of humanity is traced in gloomy colors, but the story of repeated falls is transformed into a history of salvation by the hidden providence of God who saves Noah, leads out Abraham, brings back Jacob, raises Joseph, delivers the people from Egypt and guides them in the desert. Intimate, concrete relations unite man to God who appears in human form, acts in a human manner, and feels human sentiments: Yahweh shapes man as a potter would; he walks in the garden during the cool of the evening; he accepts the hospitality of Abraham and converses with him; he is sorry and he is angry. But these anthropomorphisms[2] clothe a very elevated idea of God, who always remains the master of his creature, who does not lower himself by his care for that creature, who maintains, unimpaired, his essential holiness.

The Yahwist is keenly aware of the forces of evil at work in the world; he has no illusions about humanity and he unpityingly exposes human weakness, but he is an optimist at heart. He shows the persistence and expansion of life, the good fortune of the sons of Jacob, Israel delivered from slavery, the twelve tribes on their way to a land flowing with milk and honey. This optimism is based on a knowledge of Yahweh, on confidence in his plan and in his power.

---

2. An anthropomorphism (or 'manlikeness') is a manner of describing God or of speaking of him in human terms. It is something we cannot avoid altogether if we are to speak of him at all. Thus, though we know he is a Spirit, we can speak of the 'hand of God' and of God 'hearing' our prayers. If the Yahwist makes very free use of anthropomorphism this does not indicate a primitive notion of God, but is the expression of faith in a personal God, a God who really takes an interest in human affairs.

The *Elohistic* tradition gets its designation from the fact that it prefers the name *Elohim*—God (not a special name). It developed in Israel and was fixed in the ninth century B.C. The *Deuteronomical* tradition is confined to the Book of Deuteronomy. However, the only other (besides the Yahwistic) of the four traditions that concerns us here is the Priestly tradition which was developed by the Temple priests. Hence it is especially interested in the organization of the sanctuary, in the sacrifices and feasts, and in the persons and religious functions of Aaron and his sons. Almost all the legislation in Exodus, and all in Leviticus and Numbers, is to be attributed to this tradition. But even the narrative has a legalistic and liturgical bias. In contrast to the Yahwist the priestly writers took their stand on the transcendence of Yahweh: instead of bringing God and the word of God nearer to men they sought rather to raise man to God by fidelity to the traditional laws and prescriptions. Their rule was the command, "You shall be holy; for I Yahweh your God am holy" (Lev 19:2).

During the Babylonian Exile the deported priests, cut off from the elaborate ritual worship of Yahweh in his Temple, saw that their duty was to organize the religious life of the community in these different surroundings and circumstances. It seemed to them that the foundations on which this religious life might be built must be a common national origin, common traditions, and an authentic priesthood. Thus the priestly history took shape. The whole of it is pervaded by a theology of the divine presence and by the demands of a God of holiness.

The Yahwist

In returning to our study of marriage we shall start with the earlier Yahwistic creation-narrative (Gen 2:4b-25). Its opening verses (2:4b-6) serve as an introduction to the real purpose of the account, the formation of man; a setting has been provided but all the interest is centered in this one creature. So it first describes, vividly but briefly, the shaping of man and then depicts, at much greater length, the fashioning of woman.

> Then Yahweh God fashioned man of dust from the ground and breathed into his nostrils a breath of life, and man became a living being (2:7).

The 'dust from the ground' is fine potter's clay and the divine Potter shaped it into a human form; then he breathed into that lifeless figure a breath of life and the figure became a man. The animals, too, the narrative relates, were moulded by Yahweh and became living beings, but they were not stirred to life by the divine breath. At a later date, in the Priestly version, the reality that underlies this animation by the breath of Yahweh will be described as the making of man in the image of God. Then follows, in the text, a brief description of the garden of Eden, the first home of man, and the author goes on to the emergence of woman.

> Yahweh God said: "It is not good for man to be on his own, I will make him a helper who will suit him." Again Yahweh God fashioned from clay all the beasts of the fields and all the birds of the heavens, and he led them to the man to see what he would call them; and whatever the man called any living creature that was its name. The man gave names to all the cattle, to the birds of the heavens and to all the wild beasts; but for the man there was not found a helper that suited him.
>
> So Yahweh God caused a deep sleep to fall on the man and as he slumbered he took one of his ribs and closed up its place with flesh. Then Yahweh God built up into a woman the rib which he had taken from the man and brought her to the man. And the man exclaimed:

> "At long last, this is bone of my bone and flesh of my flesh! She shall be called 'woman' because she was taken out of man!"

That is why a man leaves his father and his mother and cleaves to his wife, and they become one flesh (2:18-24).

The philosophers tell us that man is a social animal; the Bible puts it more simply and with greater feeling: "It is not good for man to be on his own." But the inspired writer has in mind something more specific than man's gregarious instinct; he is thinking rather, of man's deep-felt need for another being like himself, one of the same nature as he, yet not quite himself. Then follows, in the text, the charming description of the parade of animals before the first man. He imposes names on all these creatures, thus, at one and the same time, manifesting his knowledge of their nature and expressing his dominion over them, because, in the biblical viewpoint, the imposition of a name implies both factors. But he can find no companion among them. Though all these creatures have been fashioned, as he was, from clay, he is unable to find one among them that can share his life, that can hold converse with him—for he alone has been livened by the divine breath.

Yahweh is still determined to provide a suitable helpmate. The fact that man and the animals are made from a common clay has not sufficed to established any real bond between them; man's helpmate must be more intimately bound to him: she will be formed from part of him. This alone will assure the desired conformity between them. It is significant that the word used, *ezer* (helper, standby) is normally applied to God himself—as in many of the psalms. So Yahweh plunges the man into a deep sleep—the Hebrew word *tardemah* means a profound and extraordinary sleep sent by God; manifestly, this is going to be an absolutely free gift. While he slept, Yahweh removed one of his ribs and proceeded to build up that rib into a woman.

This description, apparently so artless, really presents a viewpoint that is nothing less than revolutionany, especially in view of the early date of the tradition. There was a universal tendency, notably among Semites—and prevalent in Israel too despite correctives—to regard woman as a chattel and to consider her as a being definitely inferior to man. In those days it was decidedly a man's world, and the mere fact that the author took the trouble to deal specially and specifically with the creation of woman is itself significant. But he goes further than that. By describing her—in figurative terms of course—as made from man, he presents her as a being of the same nature as man, his equal; a truth which man is made to acknowledge openly (v. 22). She is, therefore, in the fullest sense, his helper, one entirely suited to him, particularly by her union with him in marriage, in which both become one flesh (v. 24).

When Yahweh introduces this new creature to him, as she stands before his delighted gaze, the man bursts into song—the first love—song! Here at last is his heart's desire, a being just like himself, one who can understand him and share his life to the full. He calls her by his own name, merely giving it a feminine form: *ishsha* from *ish*.[3] The next verse is a comment on his words. It is because they were made for each other from the beginning that man and woman will break all other ties and join in marriage. Centuries later, a greater one than the inspired writer of Genesis will add his comment and bring out the full implication of the earlier text: "So they are no longer two but one flesh. What, therefore, God has joined together let no man put asunder" (Mt 19:6).

The Priestly Writer

Though the dry, technical style of the Priestly narrative is readily recognizable, the priestly writer can sometimes reach sublime heights: his masterpiece is the creation story (Gen 1:1-2:4a). While its form and rhythm point to liturgical use, and while the re-arrangement of eight works into a six-day week points

---

3. We have here a typical Hebrew word-play: She shall be called **ishsha** because she was taken from **ish**; the etymology is popular only, it is not exact.

to pre-existing traditional material, it was surely one author who gave final form to the story. But that story is not, and is not meant to be, a scientific treatise on the origin of the world and man's beginning; rather it declares that the existence of all things and their meaning lie in God's hands. The world and everything in it has come from him, but the formation of man is his masterpiece, the pride of his creation.

> God said: "Let us make man in our image, according to our likeness, and let them have dominion over the fish of the sea, over the birds of the heavens, over the cattle, over all the wild beasts and over every creeping thing that creeps over the earth."

> God created man in his image.
> In the image of God he created him,
> Male and female he created them.

> God blessed them and said to them: "Be fruitful, multiply, fill the earth and subdue it; have dominion over the fish of the sea, over the birds of the heavens and over every living thing that moves over the earth" (1:26-28).

This description of the creation of man provides, among other things, an interesting illustration of how the Priestly writer overcame a practical difficulty. He was determined to insist on the very special nature of man's creation; the problem was, how to do it. To give him a day all to himself was out of the question because, as it was, the author's program was overcrowded: he had to fit eight works into six days. Yet, in the end, he solved it brilliantly. God who, up to now, had merely uttered his creative word, almost casually, now pauses and takes thought—"Let us make man." That is what the plural indicates, in somewhat the same way that we might remark: "Now, let us see."

The staid Priestly writer has had another surprise in store for us: most uncharacteristically he, too, breaks into song! With the account of the creation of man he has reached the climax of his creation narrative and even he is carried away by the sublimity of this last work. Man—in this account of collective noun—is created male and female, both of them in the image of God, the two sexes set on an equal footing. Thus, much more economically and just as effectively, he makes the same point as the Yahwistic author: woman is man's equal in nature and was created so from the beginning.

There is no doubt that the author has marriage in view here. It should be noted that the phrase, "Be fruitful, multiply," is a blessing, not a command. Having created the first man and woman in his image, God—by blessing them—proclaims his intention of carrying on the work begun, in them and in their descendants. Nor is this blessing one of fruitfulness only—it also involves the bringing of the earth under subjection.

"The man and woman are blessed not only in that fruitful union by which they are to fill the earth and which will give birth to the human family, but also in that union, fruitful too in its own way, by which they will *together* make the earth minister to their needs. Thus in every respect the blessing is not an individual but a common one. It is a man and woman, *by their joint activity*, who will be the masters of the 'house' bestowed by God on their race. In this way too the blessing appears once more as a correlative of the creation. What has been made in the image of God to occupy the earth and bring it into subjection is a man and a woman not isolated one from another but together. The context of the thought here, for creation as for blessing, is that of marriage and the home."[4]

The divine blessing imparted on the first pair makes it evident, once again, that the sexes are complementary and that marriage is of divine institution. It is no wonder, in view of the doctrine of these chapters, that Israel's attitude to sex and marriage was fundamentally healthy. Failures there were, because

4. J.-P. Audet, "Love and Marriage in the Old Testament", *Scripture* 10 (1958), p. 81.

man is frail—and fallen—but moral standards remained and they were exacting. It is rather the whole atmosphere that is refreshing because the thoughtful Israelite never forgot that at the end of this work God saw that it was "very good."

In the marriage of Adam and Eve we have the human prototype of marriage. The neighbors of Israel, who had created their gods in their own image, had evolved their myths in order to explain the origin of human relationships; they had their gods, and especially their goddesses of love and fertility. Israel, with its faith in only one God, could not find in him the model of human marriage, but the Israelite did believe that the Creator-God had himself instituted marriage when he created man. It is remarkable in fact that already in the tenth century B.C. monogamous marriage is proposed as the form directly established by God. It remained for the full revelation of the New Testament to show that the human prototype had, after all, a divine archetype.[5]

The Fall

If we turn again to the Yahwist we find that the story of the first human couple does not end at chap-

5. P. Grelot, **Man and Wife in Scripture** (New York: Herder & Herder, (1964), pp. 34-36.

ter 2. Immediately after his account of the creation of the first man and woman the author describes the entry of sin into the world. That first sin is not a sin of mankind in the abstract, for mankind exists only in individual men and women; it is the common sin of the first human couple.

It does not follow that the first sin was sexual in nature. Essentially, it was the transgression of a divine command, figuratively described as the prohibition to eat a certain fruit; it is significant that the tempter insinuates they will become "like divine beings who know good and evil" (3, 5). The 'knowledge of good and evil' which would be theirs, means that they would have arrogated to themselves the right to decide between good and evil, of being a law unto themselves in the moral order. Thus, in effect, they would have become independent of God. They were tempted to deny their creaturehood in the hope of transcending that condition.

What does follow is that man-woman relations were involved in the process of the sin and suffered the consequences of the fall. Woman was given to man as 'a helper fit for him' (2:18) but she became his seductress and led him into evil. Man, created before woman, was by nature her leader, yet yielding to her seduction, he weakly followed her. In place of communion in one flesh (2:24) they find complicity in crime. And when the crime had been committed the harmony that had formerly marked their relations was shattered: Adam sought to cast all the blame on Eve (3:12). But even before this they had already felt that something had gone wrong: "The eyes of both were opened and they knew that they were naked" (3:7). This is obviously meant to be seen in sharp contrast to 2:25: "Both were naked, the man and his wife, and they were not ashamed the one before the other." A shadow had fallen on sex; though good in itself, it can henceforth easily aggravate the relations between man and woman. The sentence of God: "You shall crave to have your husband, and he shall lord it over you" (3:16b) further underlines the disharmony that has been introduced. The domination of man and degradation of woman will replace the perfect union in mutual love that should have marked their relations, while fruitfulness, the normal sequel of sexual union, is set in a context of suffering: "I will greatly multiply your pain in childbearing; in pain you shall bring forth children" (3:16a). "All this is nothing other than the present condition of the human couple; man and woman, created good, have been wounded by sin and stand in need of redemption."[6]

The Yahwist's account of creation and the fall gives us, in short, an eminently realistic view of sex.

6. Ibid., p. 45.

It is a creation of God, perfectly good in itself, but fallen man is hard put to control this God-given power; for it is in this sphere, indeed, that the consequences of original sin are often most keenly felt. Yet, the state of things created by God has not collapsed hopelessly, something does remain: an institution within which love and the use of sex remain good and where fruitfulness is still a blessing. But that life of perfect happiness, which is the dream of all lovers, is no longer possible: man and woman have been driven from Eden.[7]

* * *

That vague memory of Eden is not only a dream of lovers. Creation is not a dream and God's design is not lightly set aside. The first two chapters of Genesis hold up before us the divine plan for mankind. There we can catch a glimpse of our true selves and there, too, we see an ideal of marriage that makes our romantic ideal look shoddy indeed. The rest of the Old Testament shows us sinful man and his struggle to fit together the broken fragments of the image of God; finally, God himself takes a hand, and the one perfect image of the Father comes to redeem mankind. But it is men and women who win redemption and in that

7. Ibid., p. 46.

process marriage, too, is redeemed. It falls within God's saving plan.

For God reveals himself by what he is and does and he saves men by gathering them into his plan, his 'economy'—his purpose of salvation, which is essentially historical. Salvation history is created by the word of God intervening in the course of human events; for the interventions of God are *saving* acts; God has made himself known by what he has done *for men*. To Israel, Yahweh was the God who had delivered her from Egypt and continued to save her throughout her existence. For if biblical history begins with Abraham, more exactly with God's choice of Abraham, the decisive event was several centuries later than the patriarch: this was the Exodus, the deliverance of God's people.

But the whole of the Bible is a record of salvation history; from Genesis to Apocalypse we find the impressive sweep of a great historical outline animated by the same 'economy' of God. True, the absolute limits of it go beyond history in our sense; nonetheless, Creation and Parousia (the Second Coming of Christ) are real *events*—and our picture is complete. We know how God's plan began, his design for mankind, and we know how the story will end, in the ultimate triumph of his redeeming plan. However, from Abraham to the apostolic age we have a record, guaranteed by divine authorship, of personal interventions of God in view of man's salvation, a record of his care for men. The fundamental human institution of marriage could not have escaped his solicitude. Even before the time of fulfillment, the chosen people, here too, had moved far along the road that led to Christ.

Chapter Two
Aspects of Marriage in Israel[1]

The Form

Already in the tenth century B.C. at the lastest, the Yahwistic creation narrative proposes monogamous marriage as the will of the Creator (Gen 2:21-24). In the same context the patriarchs of the line of Seth are presented as monogamous and polygamy made its appearance in the rejected line of Cain (4:19). But when we turn from the reflective reconstruction of the past (Gen 1-11) to historical times, the situation is different. True, Abraham has only one wife, Sarah —for Hagar was a concubine, not a wife—and he

---

1. This summary is based on R. de Vaux, **Les Institutions de l'Ancient Testament I** (Paris: Cerf, 1958), pp. 45-78; Eng. **tr. Ancient Israel** (London: Darton, Longman and Todd, 1961), pp. 24-42; and W. Kornfeld, "Mariage — dans l'Ancien Testament", **Dictionnaire de la Bible (Supplément)** V, 1957, cc. 906-926.

married Keturah after the death of Sarah (25:1); indeed, it seems more likely that Keturah was never more than Abraham's concubine (1 Chr 1:32). But Jacob married two sisters and Esau had three wives (Gen 29:15-30; 26:34; 28:9). At the time of the Judges (12th-11th century B.C.) we learn that Gideon had "many wives" (Jg 8:30). Finally polygamy (or, at very least, bigamy) was recognized in law (Dt 21:15-17).

Closely connected with the practice of polygamy was that of concubinage. A concubine was not a wife, nor was she regarded as such; she was, in fact, a slave. She might even be the property of a wife who had given her to her husband, especially if she, the wife, were sterile (Gen 16:2; 30:3f, 9-13), and she still remained under the authority of her mistress (16:4-6). A man's concubine might not have sexual relations with another but, apparently, she became free at his death. If she had borne him children she could not then be sold—unlike an ordinary slave. The children of a concubine were adopted by her master and were regarded as legitimate (Gen 30:3; 16:2-10), but they did not have the right of inheritance (21:10).

Despite undoubted examples of polygamy—and concubinage—it appears that monogamy was the normal practice in Israel—apart from the royal family where a large harem was a matter of prestige. It is remarkable, for instance, that the books of Samuel and Kings, which cover the whole period of the monarchy (10th to 6th centuries), record only *one* case of bigamy among commoners, and that very early —the father of Samuel (1 Sam 1:2). Similarly, the wisdom books, which give us a picture of the society of their age (5th to 1st century, B.C.), do not consider polygamy, and the many passages which regard the ideal wife are more readily understood in a strictly monogamous family (Cf. Prov 5:15-19; 31:10-31; Qoh 9:9; Sir 26:1-4). The book of Tobit, a family story, is concerned with monogamous families only. And it is in the image of a monogamous marriage that the prophets depict Israel as the only spouse of the one God. If Ezekiel does compare the relations of Yahweh with Samaria and Juda to a marriage with two sisters (Ezek 23) that is because he has developed the metaphor into an allegory and has adapted it to suit the political situation. Taking it all in all it appears that at an early stage in Israel's history the monogamous concept of marriage prevailed and, long before New Testament times ,it had become accepted as the rule.

The Institution

So much for the form; now to consider the implications of the institution. By marriage the wife became subject to her husband: he is her *ba'al*, her 'master,' just as he is the *ba'al* of a house or field (Ex 21:3, 22; 2 Sam 11:26; Prov 12:4 etc), and a married woman is the 'possession' of a *ba'al* (Gen 20:3; Dt 22:22). Does this mean that the wife was regarded as strictly the property of her husband, a mere chattel? The terminology would appear to imply as much and, added to that, the custom of the *mohar* would seem to indicate that she had been purchased by him. The *mohar* is, ordinarily, a sum of money which the fiancé had to pay to the father of the girl; it was fixed by the father (Gen 34:12) or was determined by the social position of the family (1 Sam 18:23). The payment of the *mohar* (1 Sam 18:25) could be substituted by a term of work, as for the marriages of Jacob (29:15-30) or by a service rendered, as for the marriage of David with Michal (1 Sam 18:25-27).

The obligation to pay a sum of money, or its equivalent, to the father of the fiancée obviously gives to Israelite marriage the appearance of a purchase. "But the *mohar* seems to be not so much the price paid for the woman as the compensation given to the family, and, in spite of the apparent resemblance, in law this is a different consideration. The future husband thereby acquires a right over the woman, but the woman herself is not bought and sold."[2] The difference becomes clear when the marriage with the payment of *mohar* is compared with another type of union which was indeed a purchase: a girl could be sold by her father to a man who wanted her as a concubine for himself or for his son (Ex 21:7-11) — she is a slave and not a wife.

Though the Bible gives no explicit indication, it seems that people married at an early age, very much sooner than is customary in our society. Such being the case, it is understandable that it was parents who normally arranged marriages. The girl was not consulted and, very often, the young man was not consulted either (Gen 24:33-53). The parents of the girl took the initiative and it was with them that conditions were discussed, especially the amount of the *mohar* (Gen 29:15ff; 34, 12). The words of ben-Sirach—though they have, in this context, a strangely modern ring—fitted even more aptly the society of his own time:

Unwittingly a daughter keeps her father wakeful, and worry over her robs him of sleep (Sir 42:9).[3]

2. R. de Vaux, **Ancient Israel,** (N.Y.: McGraw Hill) p. 27.

3. Translated from the Septuagint (Greek) text. The same is true of some passages of Tobit in ch. IV. All other Old Testament passages are translated from the Hebrew; all New Testament passages are translated from the Greek.

Romance

However, the authority of the parents, and their normally predominant part in marriage negotiations, does not mean that no place was left for the sentiments of the young people—love matches did occur in Israel. The young man could indicate his choice (Gen 34:4; Jg 14:2) and might even decide for himself without consulting his parents or even act contrary to their wishes (Gen 26:34-35). It is much more rare that the girl could take the initiative, like Saul's daughter Michal who fell in love with David (1 Sam 18:20).

Perhaps only the daughter of a king could afford to take direct steps but, right up to a late period of Old Testament history, mutual sentiments could not only develop but could be manifested rather easily. This was possible because, contrary to later custom, girls had considerable freedom. They looked after the flocks (Gen 29:6), went to draw water (Gen 24:13; 1 Sam 9:11), gleaned in the fields after the reapers (Ruth 2:2f) and paid visits (Gen 34:1). They could talk to men without occasioning surprise (Gen 24:15. 21; 29:11-12; 1 Sam 9:11-13. Cf. Jn 4:27).

Levirate

Still, it remains true, particularly in earlier times, that the love element had a secondary place in marriage; though even then the human affection of husband and wife was sometimes permitted to appear (Cf. Gen 24:67; 29:20, 30) and eventually, as we shall see, the balance was achieved. Yet, in the patriarchal period (19th to 16th centuries) for instance, the primary preoccupation seems to have been with fruitfulness, which is a sign of the divine blessing (15:3). Fruitfulness was valued so highly because it ensured the continuance of the tribe and of the race. It is this concern that accounts for the practice of levirate (from the Latin *levir*—brother-in-law) which, though known in the ancient Near East, was never exercised for the precise motive acknowledged in Israel (cf. Gen 38:8). According to a law of Dt 25:5-10 the provision was the following: If brothers dwelt together and one of them died without issue a surviving brother was expected to marry the widow, and the first-born son of this marriage was legally regarded as the son and heir of the deceased. The obligation might be repudiated by a declaration to that effect made before the elders and the town, but this was regarded as a dishonorable procedure (25:8-10). The custom of levirate is illustrated in the Old Testament by two examples, neither of them particularly easy to interpret—those of Tamar and Ruth.

When Judah's eldest son, Er, had died without issue (Gen 38:6f) it then became the duty of his brother Onan to marry the widow, Tamar, and "raise up offspring for his brother" (38:8). But Onan did not want to have a son who would not be legally his and, while ostensibly obeying the command of his father and fulfilling his obligation, he took care that there would be no child (38:9f). If the Lord "slew him" (38:10) it was because he had shown no concern for the well-being of his clan and so for the well-being of the family of Abraham which Yahweh had made his own; his was a sin against Yahweh himself, a breaking of the covenant. After Onan's death Judah should have given Tamar to his remaining son, Shelah, but he declined to do so (38:11). Thereupon the widow herself took drastic steps to ensure that the name of her dead husband would not perish (38:12-30).

In the story of Ruth a case of levirate is complicated by the parallel considerations of the rights of a *go'el*. The *go'el* was a redeemer, a protector, a defender of the interests of the individual and of the group (cf. Lev 25:47-49). If an Israelite had to sell his patrimony, the *go'el* had priority over all other purchasers. The levirate law of Dt 25 does not apply in the case of Ruth, for she had no more brothers-in-law (Ruth 1:11ff). "The fact that some near relative must marry her, and that this obligation proceeds in a certain order (2:20; 3:12), no doubt indicates a period or a milieu in which the law of levirate was a matter for the clan rather than for the family in the strict sense. In any case, the intention and effects of the marriage were those of a levirate marriage, for it was made "to perpetuate the name of the dead" (4:5, 10; cf 2:20) and the child born of it was considered the son of the deceased (4:6; cf 4:17).[4]

Divorce

We have remarked that in Israel, at least in later times, marriage was in practice monogamous but, to offset this, there was the problem of divorce. In Israel divorce was permitted: a husband could repudiate his wife; but the woman had no redress. (However, the *mohar*, the price which the fiancé had to pay to the father of the girl was not restored, and this was a certain safeguard). The motive accepted by Deuteronomy is "that he has found a fault to impute to her" (24:1), a very vague expression which, in rabbinical times, led to the widely divergent views of the rigoristic school of Shammai, which would admit only adultery and misconduct as valid reasons, and of the broad school of Hillel which would admit even futile reasons—that a meal had been badly prepared or that another woman was more attractive. The formality of divorce was uncomplicated; the husband made a declaration contrary to that which had

---

4. R. de Vaux, op. cit., p. 38.

concluded the marriage: "She is no longer my wife and I am no longer her husband" (Hos 2:2). Besides, he had to give the woman a bill of repudiation (Dt 24:1, 3; Is 50:1; Jer 3:8) which would allow her to remarry (Dt 24:2).

Though the law placed no restriction on a husband's right of divorce it does not seem that the right was widely exercised. The wisdom writings praise conjugal fidelity (Prov 5:15-19; Qoh 9:9) and Malachi teaches that, because marriage has made one being of the two partners, the husband should remain true to the pledge sworn to his wife:

> You cover the altar of Yahweh with your tears, with sobbing and groaning, because he no longer heeds your offering or accepts it with favor from your hand. And you ask: Why? It is because Yahweh was witness at your marriage in youth to the wife with whom you have now broken faith, though she is your companion and your wife by covenant. Has he not made them one flesh and one life? And what does that one being desire? To have children from God. Take heed then to yourselves, and let none be faithless to the wife of his youth. For I detest divorce, says Yahweh the God of Israel (Mal 2:13-16).

It is only a step to the unequivocal proclamation of the indissolubility of marriage made by Jesus, who uses, more explicitly, the same argument as Malachi: "What God has joined together, let no man separate" (Mt 19:1-9; 5:31ff).

Adultery

The onesidedness of the legislation on divorce is a reflection of a sharper lack of balance in the matter of adultery, which is viewed exclusively as an infringement of justice—of the rights of a husband. Its very place in the decalogue is significant: between murder and theft, all three being acts which injure the neighbor (Ex 20:14; Dt 5:18). As envisaged by the law, adultery is sexual intercourse of a man with a *married woman*; his own marital status is not considered, and an affair with an unmarried girl is not regarded as adultery (though it may make one subject to severe penalties on other grounds). However, the text of Lev 18:20, by bringing it within the sphere of ritual uncleanness, adds a religious consideration, and the narratives of Gen 20:1-13; 26:7-11 present adultery as a sin which God punishes—but still as a sin of injustice against one's neighbor. The law regarded adultery as a capital crime: both accomplices must be put to death (Lev 20:10; Dt. 22:22); an espoused girl (already she belonged to her fiancé) was regarded in the same light as a married woman (Dt 22:23ff). But there is not a single recorded instance of the death penalty being applied for adultery[5] and it does seem that less drastic sanctions, if any, were applied. Besides, the husband might always forgive his wife.

We may learn something more from the Book of Proverbs. The older sections of the work have few allusions to adultery (cf. 30:18-20) and appear to regard it in the same light as fornication (23:27). But the latest collection of proverbs (Chs. 1-9—perhaps 5th century B.C.) repeatedly puts young men on their guard against the seduction of a woman unfaithful to her husband. She is called the 'strange woman,' meaning simply the wife of another man (2:16-19; 5:2-14; 6:23-7:27). If her love leads to death (2:18; 5:5; 7:24-27) this 'death' is generally synonymous with moral perdition. And though there is one reference to the anger and vengeance of the offended husband (6:34) the legal penalty of adultery is never invoked. One gets the impression that this last was a dead letter, and that adultery was not uncommon. It is not surprising, then, to find conjugal fidelity strongly recommended to husbands (5:15-19). If, however, a husband were unfaithful his wife had no legal redress, while a wife guilty of miscon-

---

5. The death sentence passed on Susanna (Dan 13:41) occurs in a frankly fictional episode designed to illustrate the wisdom of the young Daniel.

duct might be repudiated and shamed (Hos 2:5, 11f; Ezek 16:37f; 23:29). Even here, husband and wife were not equal in the eyes of the law.

Status of Wife

The factor of divorce and its one-sided application, together with the concept of adultery we have just studied, raise the question of a wife's status. Juridically, in fact, a wife had few rights or none at all; but in practice her position could be very much better than her legal standing might suggest. Within the family esteem for a woman grew when she became a mother, in particular mother of a son (Gen 16:4; 29:31-30:24). Her husband became more attached to her and her children owed her respect and obedience. Not only does the decalogue (Ex 20:12) prescribe that honor must be shown to both father and mother by their children but elsewhere, too, the legislation takes care to condemn the failure of children in this duty (Ex 21:17; Lev 20:9; Dt 21:18-21; 27:16). The wisdom books also insist on the respect due to a mother (Prov 19:26; 20:20; 23:22; 30:17; Sir 3:1-16). And in the earlier narrative texts we learn of a wife being treated with love and consideration by a husband who listens to her advice and spontaneously regards her as an equal; that was the situation of the mother of Samuel (1 Sam 1:4-8, 22f), of the woman of Shunem mentioned in 2 Kg 4:8-24 and of the two older women in the Book of Tobit. And since the Old Testament has so rarely permitted us a glimpse into the intimacy of Israelite family life, we may, with some confidence, generalize from the examples cited and from a few similar texts, and feel assured that this was the normal condition. Moreover, it is in conformity with the teaching of Genesis: God had made women as a helpmate for man, one whom he should cherish (2:18, 24). The final chapter of Proverbs draws a flattering picture of the model wife, mistress of her own home, who has won for herself the blessing of her children and the praise of her husband (31:10-31). Clearly, she is a woman of maturity and poise who values her honorable status within the social limits of the times.

Motherhood

The dearest wish of an Israelite wife was to be a mother. From the start, in the patriarchal narratives, children are looked upon as the most cherished gift of God. Abraham, and then Isaac, receive the promise that their posterity will be numerous as the stars of the heavens (Gen 15:5; 22:17; 26:4). The Lord promised Hagar that she will have a posterity that cannot be numbered (16:10). Wishes uttered on the occasion of a marriage gave emphatic expression to the desire. Rebekah, on leaving her family, was blessed by her brothers: "Our sister, may you be the mother of thousands of ten thousands!" (24:60). And Boaz heard the wish that Ruth, whom he was about to marry, might be "like Rachel, and Leah who together built up the house of Israel" and that his house would flourish "with the children which the Lord will give him from this young woman" (Ruth 4:11f). Children are "the crown of the aged" (Prov 17:6), they are like "shoots of olive around the table"—and the wife is like a fruitful vine (Ps 127:3); sons are "like arrows in the hand of a warrior; happy the man who has a quiver full of them" (126:4f).

On the other hand, sterility was regarded as a trial (Gen 16:2; 30:2; 1 Sam 1:5) or as a punishment from God (20:18). It was seen as a shame of which Sarah, Rachel, and even Leah (Gen 16:2; 30:1-13) sought to be rid by adopting the child which their slaves had borne to their husbands (when given to them as concubines). Always, whether in the case of a fruitful or sterile wife, the desire was for sons who would perpetuate the name and preserve the patrimony. Daughters were less esteemed since they left the family at marriage, and it was not by their number that the strength of a house was measured.

Now, this last point, this outlook, so obviously conditioned by a particular social pattern, should warn us against raising the Israelite desire for and pride in a large family into an absolute. The social situation has changed and responsible parenthood, positively favored by the Church,[6] has become a feature of our civilization. Let us be clear that the essential biblical teaching on marriage is concerned with maintaining a truly human relationship between husband and wife and with the dignity and sanctity of family life; and while fruitfulness is candidly presented as a normal feature of marriage, the Bible as such does not regard it as the only meaning or purpose of marriage. It is surely relevant to observe that the latest writing of

6. "Let (parents) thoughtfully take into account both their own welfare and that of their cihldren, those already born and those which the future may bring. For this accounting they need to reckon with both the material and the spiritual conditions of the times as well as of their state in life. Finally, they should consult the interests of the family group, of temporal society, and of the Church herself. The parents themselves and no one else should ultimately make their judgment in the sight of God, but in their manner of acting, spouses should be aware that they cannot proceed arbitrarily, but must always be governed according to a conscience dutifully conformed to the divine law itself, and should be submissive towards the Church's teaching office, which authentically interprets the law in the light of the Gospel." Vatican Council II: **Pastoral Constitution on the Church in the Modern World**, Part II, Ch. I, par. 50.

"In keeping with man's inalienable right to marry and generate children, a decision concerning the number of children they will have depends on the right judgment of the parents." Ibid. Part II, ch. V, par. 87.

the Old Testament, the Book of Wisdom, disagrees sharply with the glorification of a large family on the mere basis of number. The passage 3:10-4:6 points out that 'the barren woman who is undefiled' and the "eunuch whose hands have done no lawless deed" are blessed in the sight of the Lord, while the ungodly reap no profit from a large progeny. The virtuous barren wife will "have fruit when God examines souls" and eunuch who lives justly will have "a place of great delight in the temple of the Lord."

Mixed Marriages

The question of mixed marriages is not a modern one only; it was known in Israel and had become a crucial problem in the period of re-settlement after the Exile. Already, a little earlier than that, Deuteronomy had opposed mixed marriages, on religious grounds: the people of Yahweh would be turned away, by their pagan wives or husbands, from following him (7:3f). A more fundamental danger, with grave consequences for the future, was that the children of such unions would no longer be educated in Yahwism and live according to the commandments of the covenant; they would not be the godly offspring which God desired for his people (Mal 2:15). By his criticism of mixed marriages (Mal 2:10-16) the post-exilic prophet hit at current abuses and anticipated the reforms of Nehemiah and Ezra. These men, the founders of post-exilic Judaism, took a radical stand against mixed marriages. The problem had arisen because the majority of those who had returned from Babylon were men, and they had sought wives for themselves among their Palestinian neighbors; now the reformers decreed that the foreign wives must be divorced and their children sent away (cf. Neh 13:1-3, 23-27; 10:31; Ez 9). A religious motive (Ez 9:1, 11) was invoked to justify such extreme measures.

The basic and essential dogmatic meaning of this Old Testament vision is undoubtedly that faithfulness to God takes precedence, even in marriage, should this ever lead to infidelity in religion; and moreover that in a mixed marriage it is a grave matter of conscience for the parents to bring up the children in this religion. How this duty was to be reconciled with the conscience of the other party in a mixed marriage is a problem which was not posed in Israel; it is a problem which has arisen out of modern man's sensitivity towards the validity of his fellow-men's convictions.[7]

7. E. Schillebeeckx, **Marriage: Secular Reality and Saving Mystery I.** (N.Y.: Sheed & Ward, 1966), p. 146.

But another factor also entered in, that of purity of blood or racialism. In the tiny Jewish state the struggle to preserve national identity was a painful one. Some had come to regard mixed marriages as a mortal danger to the continued existence of the people as the people of God; an excessively nationalistic and exclusive outlook tended to develop. The author of the little Book of Ruth struck a blow on behalf of a more liberal and more universalist outlook. Ruth the Moabitess (a foreigner) had accepted Yahweh as her God (Ruth 1:16) and had entered so wholeheartedly into the Jewish way of life that she was lauded by Boaz for her earnestness in seeking the one kind of marriage that would perpetuate the family name. The divine favor came upon her: she had become an ancestress of David, a mother of the Messianic family.

The Ceremonies

An Israelite marriage was normally preceded by a promise of marriage—engagement, or betrothal—made some time before the celebration of the marriage. Though Hebrew had a special word for the custom we are given little information about it in the Bible. The cases of Isaac and Jacob (Gen 29:15-21) are special. David was betrothed to Merab, but when the wedding should have taken place, she was given to another (1 Sam 18:17-19). Then Michal was betrothed to him and did become his wife (18:26f). On the other hand, Tobias married Sarah at their first meeting, just as soon as the terms of the marriage contract could be arranged (Tob 7:9-16). Betrothal, in its juridical consequences, went far beyond our engagement—which is no more than a private agreement. In Israel, a girl engaged to be married belonged to her fiancé in the same way as a married woman belonged to her husband (cf. Dt 20:7; 22:23-27).

It is important to realize that in Israel—as in Mesopotamia—marriage was a purely civil contract (and a private, not a public contract) and was not sanctioned by any religious ceremony. However, only in Tobit (7:13) do we explicitly hear of a written marriage contract. But we do possess many such contracts from the Jewish colony of Elephantine (in Egypt on an island in the Nile opposite Aswan) dating from the fifth century B.C., and the custom was firmly established among the Jews in the Graeco-Roman era. It must have been in vogue earlier than the fifth century because acts of divorce were drawn up before the Exile (Dt 24:1, 3; Jer 3:8), and it would be surprising if marriage contracts had not existed at the same time. The marriage formula occurs in the Elephantine texts. The husband declared: "She is my

wife and I am her husband, from this day and forever"; the woman made no declaration (cf. Tob
7:11).

Marriage was an occasion for rejoicing. The chief
ceremony was the entry of the bride into the home
of her future husband. The bridegroom, wearing a
diadem (Song 3:11, Is 61:10), and accompanied by
his friends, went to the bride's house. She was richly
apparelled (Ps 44:14f; Is 61:10) but veiled (Song
4:1, 3; 6:7). She unveiled only in the bridal chamber
—this explains how Laban was able to substitute
Leah for Rachel at Jacob's first marriage (Gen 29:23-
25). Then, accompanied by her friends, the bride
was led to the home of the bridegroom. Love songs
were sung (Jer 16:9) in praise of the young couple
(cf. Ps 44; Song). A feast followed (Gen 29:22; Jg
14:10; Tob 7:14), normally lasting seven days. But
the marriage was consummated on the first night
(Gen 29:23; Tob 8:1).

Israelite Attitude to Sex

From what we have seen of the approach to marriage it is clear that the Israelite outlook was fundamentally healthy. Like their contempories, the Hebrews tended to attribute a sacred character to everything which touches life, sex and fecundity, but the

manner in which they did so marks their religious distinctiveness. In ancient Semitic religions the myth and ritual of fertility occupied the central place. The Canaanite religion (which most closely affected Israel) was a fertility cult. Head of the Canaanite pantheon was El, but the chief active deity was Ba'al (Lord). Female deities, variously named Asherah, Astarte, Anat, represented the female principle in the fertility cult. A central element of Canaanite myth was the death and resurrection of Ba'al, corresponding to the annual death and resurrection of nature. In this context such rites as sacred prostitution become understandable: by sexual union at the shrine the union of god and goddess was re-enacted, and, by a sort of sympathetic magic, the desired fertility of man, beast and soil was secured. Though the Bible vehemently condemns it, the Canaanite religion continued to have a powerful fascination for the Hebrews, especially when they had settled down to agricultural life.

The authentic Israelite view of the sacredness of sex shows itself (apart from the high regard for marriage) in certain legal prescriptions. To understand these it is necessary to consider the general context of Lev 11-15, which has to do with 'cleanness' and 'uncleanness.' The various rules put forward in these chapters stem from very old religious prescriptions: whatever can come near God is clean; whatever is excluded from the cult or renders one unsuited for participation in it is unclean. Clean animals are those which can be sacrificed to God. Some animals are unclean (taboo) because they were sacred to other gods, some because they were repulsive in looks or habits and so regarded as repugnant to God. Other rules touch on birth, sexual life and death: mysterious domains where God, master of life, acts. So, all blood was taboo and all issues of blood are always unclean. Uncleanness, by itself, has nothing to do with morality. An action morally good—like the burial of the dead which is an act of piety (Lev 21:1-3) or a work of charity (Tob 2:1, 9) renders one unclean. For a woman children are an honor and a blessing (1 Sam 1:6) and yet childbirth renders her unclean (Lev 12). In Semitic religions, especially in that of the Old Testament, the unclean is determined by relation to the divinity (cf. Lev 15:31): it is that which prevents a man from approaching God. Uncleanness cuts one off from Yahweh and his cult.

This has nothing to do with ethical matters, but with ritual cleanness and uncleanness. 'Holy' is that which has to do with God, and everything that belongs to God is 'holy.' Uncleanness has to do partly with the preservation of society and partly with the other world of spirits and taboos. The Hebrews acted on the theory that God is concerned with every aspect of life and with the whole of it, and this led them to bring all these primitive laws, based on early natural religion, within their religious system. Thus rules which, as a sanitary necessity, involved exclusion from the community (e.g. leprosy), also involved exclusion from worshipping God within the post-exilic religious community. (Much of the legislation of Lev is post-exilic.) Being cut off from the people involved also being cut off from God.[8]

Against this general background we may now appreciate more easily—and more sympathetically—the meaning of a few texts that might seem to cast a certain shadow on Israel's essentially healthy view of marriage. The short section Lev 12:1-8 introduces temporary cases of ritual impurity by means of the principal among them: childbirth. Other peoples also regarded childbirth as a cause of uncleanness; just like the menstrual flow or emission of semen (Lev 15:16) it was regarded as a loss of vitality by the individual who must, by certain rites, regain his integrity and his union with the divinity, with the living God who is the source of life. Taboos on women in childbirth are common among primitive peoples, and the rules given in Leviticus are survivals. The custom also is common of observing a longer period for girls than for boys, it being held that the birth of a girl is more dangerous

---

8. N. H. Snaith, **Peake's Commentary on the Bible** (edd. Black & Rowley; London: Nelson, 1962), 207a.

than that of a boy. The menstrual period is the time in which the source of blood, therefore of life, is particularly exposed; it must therefore be the more respected (Lev 20:18). So, during the time of menstruation (Lev 15:25), and also doubtless during the time after childbirth, sexual intercourse was forbidden.

Turning from the aspect of vitality to that of the cult, we find the principle that sexual intercourse rendered one unfit for any sacred sexual intercourse prescribed during military campaigns (1 Sam 21:5; 2 Sam 11:11), since the people in arms must be in a state of ritual cleanness. War was a sacred enterprise and consequently, in order to take part in it, it was necessary—as for participation in a religious act—to be free from all uncleanness (no matter how involuntarily incurred) (Dt 23:9-11).

At the risk of becoming tedious we must emphasize once again that ritual 'uncleanness' carried with it no implication of moral guilt. And we must certainly not imagine that the Hebrews regarded sexual intercourse and childbirth as in some way shameful or in any degree tainting—any suggestion of Victorianism would be quite foreign to their attitude. But they were people of their own time and environment and had inherited, from the distant past, a number of religious taboos. It is true that these were never wholly integrated into their way of life and conflicted in some measure with a more developed and mature mentality. Also, as so often happens, such practices were simply observed without knowledge of their origin and with little or no realization of their real meaning.[9] It would appear, then, that the Levitical restrictions underline the sacredness of sex. When properly understood they do not conflict with the general biblical outlook on sexuality and marriage. But they do, obviously, point to a responsible and disciplined approach to the use of sex.

Perhaps we are already aware that, though we cannot expect to encounter specifically Christian values, we have something to learn from the people of Israel. And as we turn from a study of the outward form of marriage to a consideration of its more profound aspect we shall find that the Old Testament has much to teach us Christians.[10]

---

9. We might compare our 'churching' ceremony before the recently revised ritual had clarified its meaning and purpose. It seems that there was widespread misapprehension of the significance of the rite — and yet mothers eagerly availed themselves of it.

10. "Now the books of the Old Testament, in accordance with the state of mankind before the time of salvation established by Christ, reveal to all men the knowledge of God and of man and the ways in which God, just and merciful, deals with men. These books, though they also contain some things which are incomplete and temporary, nevertheless show us true divine pedagogy." Vatican Council II: **Dogmatic Constitution on Divine Revelation**, ch. IV, par. 15.

Chapter Three
The Prophetic Image

Marriage fits into the plan of God's creation and stands under his care and protection! This realization is evident in the Yahwistic creation-narrative. Eventually the idea emerged that marriage was the means of revealing the community and the complex relationship existing between Yahweh and his people. So it was that the human experience of marriage won a new dignity as a result of a prophetical theme, one which seems to have originated with Hosea and which was developed by him. He it was who, for the first time, represented the covenant relation of Yahweh with his people as a marriage. It would, of course, have seemed natural enough that the covenant, a treaty between God and Israel, might have been likened to the marriage contract between man and wife. The singular fact is that it is not the contract aspect that was exploited but, rather, the love aspect, and especially the love of a husband for his wife.

The Covenant

It is well to have a clear idea of the prophetic image and what it involves; and this means that we must first explain the idea and nature of the covenant. To express the nature of the link which exists between God and his people the Old Testament uses the word *berith* (rendered in Greek by *diathēkē* and in Latin by *testamentum*). In English it is generally translated as 'covenant.' The term 'covenant,' which in its technical theological sense concerns the relations of man with God, was borrowed from the social experience of men, from the fact of treaties and alliances between peoples and individuals. In practice, the religious use of the term regards a special type of covenant, that in which one partner takes the initiative and imposes the conditions. Therefore God lays down the terms, demands of his people that they should keep the covenant, while he binds himself by promise. It was not primarily an assertion of power and authority on the part of Yahweh but an expression of his *hesed*, his steadfast love.

But the saving covenant of Yahweh and Israel, like every other reality of revelation, had to be expressed in human terms. And when they seized on married life, with its ups and downs, as a revealing reflection of the relations between God and his people, the prophets were not directly concerned with marriage;

they had no intention of casting fresh light on marriage. It was their concern to illustrate the *hesed* of Yahweh and his desire that his love should be reciprocated, to sketch a theology of grace and salvation. Inevitably, though, their imagery must have added a new depth to the concept of human marriage.

Hosea

Indeed, this aspect is already apparent in the marriage of Hosea for, from his own experience, he realized the aptness of the marriage image to describe the relations between Yahweh and his people. In the opening chapters of his book the prophet has given us a sketch of his painful family life: his marriage is described in biographical style (Hos 1) and in autobiographical style (Hos 3). From this arrangement two questions emerge: Do chapters 1 and 3 represent successive stages of the prophet's experience with one woman, Gomer? Is the woman of chapter 3—she is unnamed—another woman and not Gomer? If the second alternative is correct, then chapter one describes the real marriage and chapter 3 is the description of a prophetic symbol: the purchase and seclusion of a cult-prostitute as a symbol of God's plan for his unfaithful people.

It is much more probable that both chapters recount Hosea's experience with Gomer, for if the woman of chapter 3 were another we should expect more explicit mention of it. The analogy with Israel (Hos 3:1b) suggests that the prophet is to be reconciled with Gomer, just as Yahweh will take back to himself the Israel he had rejected. "In chapter 1 the theme is the faithlessness of Israel; in chapter 3 it is the steadfastness of Yahweh's love in the face of infidelity. These themes are not based on one event of Hosea's life, but on a sequence of events in his relations with Gomer."[1]

In the second chapter the symbolism of the marriage is worked out. The contract element and the matter of fruitfulness are not considered at all, but only the love aspect, for it is seen that the psychology of human love can wonderfully illustrate the mystery of God's relations with men, the reality and depth of his love. The divine Husband has been betrayed by his wife who has given herself to adultery and prostitution. Yet he seeks only to win her again to him, and if he chastises her it is with that sole end in view. As a last resort he determines to bring her back once more to the conditions of the Exodus, the honeymoon period of their love:

> Therefore, behold, I will allure her,
>   and lead her into the desert,

---

1. B. W. Anderson, **The Living World of the Old Testament** (London: Longmans, 1958), p. 242.

> and speak to her heart . . .
> There she shall make answer as in the days of
>   her youth,
>   as on the day when she came out of the land
>   of Egypt (2:16f).

In fact, he ultimately goes beyond this and promises to bring her into the harmony of a new garden of Eden (2:18) where their love will be the crowning and fulfillment of the mutual love of the first human couple:

> I will betroth you to me forever,
> I will betroth you to me in righteousness and
>   in justice,
>   in kindness and in love.
> I will betroth you to me in faithfulness,
>   and you shall know Yahweh (2:21f).

Later Prophets

The theme of God's love for his people is already fully developed in Hosea and later prophets do little more than ring the changes on it. The first presentation of the image in Jeremiah (2:1-4:4) opens with the poignant recall of a promising beginning:

> I remember the devotion of your youth,
>   the love of your bridal days;

> How you followed me in the wilderness,
>   in a land unsown (2:2).

The rest is a sad catalogue of perversities interspersed with the passionate pleadings of a loving God. But his tenderest words are reserved for the moment of despair when the people, deaf to his warnings and blind to his guidance, have rushed unheedingly into disaster and find themselves exiles from a ravaged homeland. Now is the moment when he utters words of loving consolation:

> I have loved you with an everlasting love,
>   and so I have held out my kindness to you;
> Once more I will build you, and you shall be
>   built,
> O virgin Israel! (31:3f).

He has remained faithful, unchanging, in spite of everything. And in the end he gently chides his people for their tardiness in realizing that he loves them still and that he is welcoming them back to him:

> Return, O virgin Israel,
>   return to these your cities.
> How long will you go hither and thither,
>   O erring daughter?

> For Yahweh has created a new thing on the earth:
>
> the woman seeks out her husband[2] (31:21f).

The return of Israel to her Husband will be a 'new thing,' a miracle of grace. That return is to be seen in the perspective of the New Covenant foretold in the same chapter (31:31-34). It is within this New Covenant that marriage too will come into its own and, now a source of grace, will sanctify men and women of the new Israel and lead them to their God.

Ezekiel has developed the same theme in two long allegories (Ezek 16:23) which, however, lack the poetry of Hosea and Jeremiah. In Chapter 23 the legal recognition of bigamy is exploited in the presentation of the conduct and punishment of the two sisters, Samaria and Jerusalem, unfaithful wives of God, and the prophet emphasizes the justice of a loving God who cannot allow his love to be forever trodden underfoot.

With Second Isaiah we return to the spirit of Hosea (Is 54:1-10). The Israel of the Exile, a barren woman separated from her husband (vv. 1, 6) will now, at the glad return, rejoice again at Yahweh's

---

2. V. 22 is uncertain in the Hebrew. The **Bible de Jerusalem** rendering has been followed: **le Femme recherche son Mari.**

wife and be comforted by many children (vv. 1-3).
It is the final triumph of God's love:

> Fear not, for you will not be put to shame;
>> be not confounded, for you will not be put
>> to the blush.
> For the shame of your youth you will forget,
>> and the reproach of your widowhood you
>> will remember no more.
> For your Husband is your Maker,
>> Yahweh of hosts is his name;
> Your Redeemer is the Holy One of Israel,
>> the God of all the earth he is called.
> As a wife forsaken and grieved in spirit
>> Yahweh has called you.
> Does one cast off the wife of his youth?
>> asks your God.
> For a brief moment have I forsaken you,
>> but with great compassion will I gather you;
> In overflowing wrath, for a moment, I hid my
>> face from you,
>> but with everlasting love will I have pity on
>> you,
>> says Yahweh, your Redeemer . . .
> For the mountains may depart
>> and the hills be shaken;
> But my love shall not depart from you,

and my covenant of peace will not be
shaken,
says Yahweh, who pities you (54:4-8, 10).

But, after all, this cannot be only the Jerusalem of the
Return, the scene of the eventual crucifixion of the
Messiah. "The ideal Spouse of Yahweh is no longer
the historical people of Israel, it is redeemed humanity.
In the figure world of the Old Testament, the espousals of Sinai only foreshadows the final espousals
of the last age."[3]

This sketch gives an inkling of the prophets' use
of the marriage image to portray God's attitude towards his people. Even if we were to regard it as no
more than imagery we must admit that, granted their
elevated notion of God, it witnesses to the prophets'
high esteem of marriage; otherwise they would never
have used the image in this context. But it seems that
we can, and ought, admit that marriage, ever since
it had become a means of revealing the covenant between God and Israel, has taken on a fresh dimen-
sion. Edward Schillebeeckx writes:

Revealing his covenant through the medium of
human marriage, God simultaneously revealed to
men a meaning of marriage which they had not

3. P. Grelot, op. cit., pp. 57 f.

hitherto suspected. He did not do this by means of a separate revelation, but by revealing himself in marriage and thus setting it in a 'luminous circle' so that it became transparent and was sanctified by the God of salvation. The covenant of salvation was not revealed to us by means of some abstract concept, but through a fact of human existence. . . . Conversely the transcendental, 'sacramental' value of the secular reality of marriage became capable of penetration by us men. However, this did not become fully possible until divine revelation was fulfilled in Christ.[4]

In conclusion we may observe that among the many things we may learn from the people of the Old Testament not the least is the realization that *everything* God has made is good. This is true of marriage, as God planned it, and it is true, within God's purpose, of human love.

4. E. Schillebeeckx, op. cit.,

Chapter Four
Personal Values

Though the prophetic image had stressed the love element in marriage, the fact does not appear to have had any immediate repercussions. For one thing it remained an exclusively prophetical theme and does not appear in the Wisdom literature or in the other later Old Testament books. Yet, we may believe that its influence had made itself felt, if in a subtle way. At any rate the sages can speak in glowing terms of married bliss: "Find your joy in the wife of your youth— a lovely hind, a charming doe. Let her affection enrapture you, be infatuated always with her love" (Prov 5:18f; cf. 12:4; 31:10-31). A happy marriage is a blessing from God: "He who finds a good wife finds a fortune—a favor bestowed by Yahweh" (18:22; cf. 19:14). When he has noted that the third of three things which delight him is "a wife and husband who live in harmony" (Sir 25:1), Ben Sirach goes on to

paint parallel portraits of the evil wife and the good
wife (25:13-26:18). He, too, counts a good wife as
a great blessing and refers to the happiness of a man
who has found such a treasure. Yet, like most of the
wisdom writers, he is something of a misogynist:
"From a woman sin had its beginning, and because of
her we all die" (25:24; cf. 25:16, 19; 26:6; 42:13f).
In this twofold attitude which sees her as the helpmate or the temptress, we see a reflection of the Yahwistic narrative in which Eve is both the one and the
other (cf. Gen 2:18; 3:6).

Mutual Love

In post-exilic Judaism desire for a posterity was
still dominant. This was a situation which might seem
to lead to a rather one-sided conception of husband
and wife relations in which mutual love and tenderness would find little part. If this ever had been so it
is certain that the balance was eventually restored. Indeed, we catch stray glimpses of tenderness even in
an earlier age: Jacob and Rachel (Gen 29:18-20),
Michal and David (1 Sam 18:20) and Elkanah, the
father of Samuel, who comforted his barren wife:
"Hannah, why do you weep? And why do you not
eat? And why is your heart sad? Am I not more to
you than ten sons?" (1:8).

For, if the fruitfulness of marriage is the aspect of it that is principally stressed, the personal relations of love and affection, which bind husband and wife, are an integral part of it. The reaction of the first man when confronted with his partner was one of spontaneous joy—it was literally love at first sight. It is not for the sole purpose of procreating and bringing up children that a man and woman will break all other ties and live together for a lifetime as the Genesis text implies. The love that is normally an ingredient of married life, and which ought to be present at all times, is part of the work that God has made and has called very good.

Now this aspect of marriage, which tended to be minimized, is—at least according to a widely-held interpretation of the book—the special theme of the Song of Songs. It is true that the Song has long been regarded as an allegory, immediately signifying the union of Yahweh with Israel; and this is a factor which cannot simply be ignored.

Divine Love?

The allegorical interpretation has been dominant among Jews and Christians; in recent years it has been warmly and competently presented by eminent scholars.[1] Both as a traditional view and on the basis of scholarship it merits serious attention, and yet, on both grounds, it is vulnerable. For one thing, it seems that the earliest evidence we have in support of the allegorical interpretation is a second-century A.D. Jewish tradition.[2] The Song was accepted as part of the Jewish canon (that is, as Scripture) not because it was regarded as an allegory but because of its popularity. On the other hand, this interpretation demands that too much should be read into the text. For instance, the historical and topographical significance attributed to descriptive details is forced and seems arbitrary.[3]

Perhaps the most serious difficulty is that nothing in these poems suggests that they are allegories. Elsewhere (as in Hos, Jer, Ezek), where nuptial language is used to describe the relationship between Yahweh and his people, the allegorical nature of the language is always made clear. It is noteworthy too that when

1. See A. Robert, Le Cantique des Cantiques (BJ) (Paris: Cerf, 1958²); A. Feuillet, Le Cantique des Cantiques (Paris: Cerf, 1953); A. Robert et R. Tournay (avec le concours de A. Feuillet), Le Cantique des Cantiques (Paris: Gabalda, 1963).

2. See J.-P. Audet, "Le sens du Cantique des Cantiques", Revue Biblique, 62 (1955), pp. 200-203; "Love and Marriage in the Old Testament", Scripture, 10 (1958), p. 81.

3. See, for example, A. Robert (BJ). The sustained interpretation is a brilliant tour de force; one is impressed but not convinced.

the biblical writers have written of Yahweh and his people in marital terms, they have displayed an obvious restraint and have set definite limits to the imagery; the boldness of the Song's language would surely strike the earlier writers as out of place in the context. Besides, the marriage image is a prophetical theme, whereas the Song of Songs is lyric poetry and —as it is presented by its editors—belongs to the wisdom literature. All in all, despite its long tradition and eminent champions, the allegorical interpretation of the Song is difficult to maintain. We turn, by choice, to the literal interpretation .

Human Love?

The literal interpretation takes the Song at its face value, regarding it as a love poem or a collection of love poems celebrating the love of a man and a woman. It has been urged in the past—and the prejudice still lingers—that the theme of human love is unworthy of Scripture; or, at least, that it is unlikely, unseemly even, that a biblical book should have been wholly dedicated to it. This outlook would appear to miss the true significance of Scripture. The Bible is the word of God, certainly, but (we may ask) to whom is that word addressed? God has not had this book written just for his own pleasure; he has destined it for the human beings whom he had created;

it is his gift to them. It is he who has made them men and women; it is he who has implanted in them, deep in their nature, the mutual attraction that is meant to culminate in marriage. Like all the gifts of God this may be abused but, in the divine intention, the love which so strongly draws young people, which inspires each of them to dedicate his and her life to the other, and which later enables them, together, to support inevitable cares and troubles, is a good thing —it is part of the work which God himself called good (Gen 1:31). It is eminently worthy of special treatment in the Bible, that word of God *to men.*

In Praise of Love

The Song of Songs takes its place in the Bible as the exaltation of human love. Whether it is a collection of songs, or whether it is one elaborate poem (the unity of authorship seems to be undeniable), it is certainly lyrical: as such it does not 'teach,' it has no 'doctrine' to propound—it is the expression of a state of mind and heart. It is concerned with the mutual love of two young people who quite obviously contemplate marriage if, indeed, they are not already married. The language of it, throughout, is the language of love and if it seems daring to our Western ears, perhaps at times even shocking in its realism, that is because it is the product of another culture. It is surely relevant to note that throughout the Old Testament the same Hebrew verb and noun are used for human and divine love,[4] but when we turn to the New Testament we find that the Christian authors writing in Greek, could not use the ordinary word for love in their religious vocabulary because its association had made it unfit for such usage.[5] The same is very nearly the case today when 'love' is so often a synonym of 'lust.'

We are not sure when the Song originated but we may say that it was edited by wisdom writers after the Exile, most likely in the fourth-century B.C. The epilogue of the poem (or an editorial addition) would indicate that the author (certainly the editors) understood the writing in its straightforward literal sense:

> For love is strong as death,
>   jealousy is cruel as Sheol.
> Its flashes are flashes of fire,
>   a very flame of Yahweh.
> Many waters cannot quench love,
>   nor can floods drown it.

---

4. See A.-M. Dubarle, "L'Amour humain dans le Cantique des Cantiques" **Revue Biblique,** 61 (1954), pp. 67-86; J.-P. Audet, op. cit; J. Winandy, **Le Cantique des Cantiques** (Paris: Ed. de Maredsous, 1960).

5. See A. S. Herbert, **Peake's Commentary on the Bible,** pp. 469 f.

> If a man should offer all the wealth of his house
>> as a price for love,
> he would be utterly scorned (8, 6b-7).[6]

Such language is reminiscent of Proverbs or Sirach and orientates the Song in the traditional direction of wisdom literature;[7] the writing was reinterpreted in terms of the mutual love of Yahweh and Israel only after the book had taken its place in the canon. The growing tendency among Catholic scholars to read the Canticle according to its obvious sense is due to the realization that the theme of human love is no more out of place in the wisdom literature than is the theme of human wisdom in Proverbs.

* * *

A feature of the Song that often occasions surprise is the absence of the divine Name. What should really surprise us is the absence of any allusion to a god or goddess of love. Israel did indeed feel the strong attraction of the *Ashtaroth* (the Canaanite god-

---

6. A renowned scholar comments: "Nowhere in the entire range of world literature can we find an equal to the praise of the love of man for woman in Canticle 8:6 f." W. F. Albright, **Archaeology and the Religion of Israel** (Baltimore: John Hopkins Press, 1964), p. 23.

7. For the same theme as that of the Song see Prov. 5:15-19; 31:10-31; Sir. 25:13-26:18.

desses of fertility) and did fall into idolatry, but Israel itself never divinized love, it never even personified love. The explanation of this fact, which is truly remarkable when we view it in historical perspective, is to be found in the second chapter of Genesis. There is no essential difference between the admiration that attracted the first man to the first woman (Gen 2:23) and the mutual wonder of the young couple of the Song. There is little difference between the comment of the editor of Genesis: "That is why a man leaves father and mother and cleaves to his wife, and they become one flesh" (2:24) and the reflection of the poet (or editor) of the Song: "For love is strong as death. . . . If a man should offer all the wealth of his house as a price for love, it would be utterly scorned" (8:6f). Both texts bear witness to the same attitude in face of the same human experience. Marital love belongs to the order of things created by God from the beginning. It is one of the wonders of God which should evoke admiration and gratitude.[8]

8. See J.-P. Audet, "Le Sens du Cantique des Cantiques", pp. 219-220. "This love is an eminently human one since it is directed from one person to another through an affection of the will; it invokes the good of the whole person, and therefore can enrich the expressions of body and mind with a unique dignity, ennobling these expressions as special ingredients and signs of the friendship distinctive of marriage. This love God

It is arguable that the Song was originally a collection of espousal songs or songs of the wedding feast; at least it has been inspired and colored by such songs. This explains the atmosphere of it, the springtime joy, the companions, and the young couple immersed in each other. The whole is admittedly on a natural plane, but is there anything reprehensible in that? Love is normally awakened by physical beauty, by very human qualities, and God made man's body as well as man's soul. It would be unrealistic, to say the least of it, to seek to ignore all this; logically it would lead to a denial of the role of sex in marriage. Besides (and this is more to the point) such an attitude is entirely unbiblical.

In the biblical view there never is an obligation which has not been preceded by a corresponding gift of God. It is because Yahweh has delivered his people from Egypt that Israel is obliged to

has judged worthy of special gifts, healing, perfecting and exalting gifts of grace and of charity. Such love, merging the human with the divine, leads the spouses to a free and mutal gift of themselves, a gift proving itself by gentle affection and by deed; such love pervades the whole of their lives: indeed by its busy generosity it grows better and grows greater."
Vatican Council II, **Pastoral Constitution on the Church in the Modern World**, Part II, Ch. I, par. 49.

adore him alone (Ex 20:2f; Dt 5:6f). In the same way the overflowing happiness of the Canticle, a happiness which will be doled out more sparingly afterwards, is the divine gift which prompts the acceptance of future duties: daily work, painful maternity, persevering faithfulness. A passage which can well be the climax of the work begins with an adjuration and then goes on to formulate, in more abstract terms, the practical conclusion of the poems: unshakable fidelity is the very expression of true love—and this is not a matter of social constraint; it is the inevitable desire of a heart entirely given to another (8:6f).

The spontaneous accord of two young people is a more striking introduction to the wonderful harmony of the work of God than is the mutual understanding patiently acquired by the sharing of good and ill over the course of a long life. The joy of love newborn gives a taste of creation in its first unblemished beginning. . . . It is not by chance that these love poems are accompanied by a feeling for all that is gracious and charming in nature more vivid than anywhere else in the Old Testament and which has been equalled only by the Gospel (Mt 6:29; 23:27).[9]

9. A.-M. Dubarle, art. cit., pp. 82 f.

Personal Values

There is yet another point that is well worth noting. By attracting attention to the personal element in marriage the Song has not merely provided a more balanced view but has enriched the concept of marriage. Love brings out the unique value of the person (cf. Song 2:2f; 5, 10; 6, 8f) and establishes a real equality between man and woman. It is significant that the latter's freedom of choice is here quite obviously taken for granted. Perhaps even more striking is the fact that, in the context, anything other than a monogamous and indissoluble union would be unthinkable.

But there is still more of it. The important fact that a biblical writing has extolled the tender love of a young couple not only restores the balance of marriage but has its place in the development of revelation.[10] It plays its part in the transformation of the essentially communitary covenant of Sinai into the New Covenant foretold by Jeremiah (31:31-34), a covenant in which the place and dignity of the individual are explicitly affirmed. For, when love has been acknowledged as a constitutive element in marriage side by side with the founding of a family, the individual has ceased to be absorbed in the group.

10. Ibid., p. 84.

It is a decisive step towards the recognition of the personal dignity of every man and woman.

Tobias and Sarah

The charming story of Tobit—itself largely inspired by biblical models, especially by the patriarchal narratives of Genesis: Abraham and Sarah, Isaac and Rebekah, Jacob and Rachel—forms a fitting pendant to the Song of Songs. Here too, in the romance of Tobias and Sarah, the love theme is very much to the fore. Tobias loved his future wife even before he had set eyes on her. The angel told him of Sarah and indicated that she had been destined for him from eternity, and when he had heard all this "he fell deeply in love with her and lost his heart to her hopelessly" (Tob 6:17). It is really love in the truest and finest sense, and the writer is at pains to put the matter beyond doubt. He tells us that on the wedding night Tobias was formally conducted, by the parents of Sarah, to the bridal chamber. And straightway, when the door had been shut and the two were alone:

> Tobias rose up from the bed and said to her: "Sister, arise, let us pray and have recourse to our Lord that he may have mercy on us and protect us." So she arose and they began to pray and to beseech the divine protection. And Tobias began:

Blessed are you, O God of our fathers,
and blessed is your Name for ever and ever!
Let the heavens bless you, and all your
    creatures,
for ever and ever!
You it is who made Adam,
and you it is who made Eve his wife
as his helper and his support:
from both of them the race of man has sprung.
You it is who said:
"It is not good that the man should be alone,
let us make him a helper like unto him."
And now I take not this my sister because of
    lust,
but in sincerity;
Grant that I and she may find mercy,
and may grow old together.

And they said in unison: "Amen, amen!" Then
they went to sleep for the night (8:4-10).[11]

It is not surprising that our marriage liturgy is
colored by the book of Tobit, for Tobias and Sarah
do indeed stand as an example to Christian husbands
and wives. And in the same writing we see that a

---

11. The translation follows the Greek text of the fourth
century A.D. **Codex Sinaiticus,** which differs notably from the
more familiar text.

deeply religious concept of marriage goes hand in hand with the realization that a marriage is a happy occasion to be celebrated with joy and gladness (8:19-21; 11:17f). Just such a wedding-feast was sanctified by the presence of our Lord himself, who indeed worked his first miracle that a shortage of wine should not mar the joy of the feast (Jn 2:1-11). But he was not content only to grace a village wedding with his presence and thus set his seal of approval on a very human institution. He who had come not to abolish but to perfect, here too, went beyond the Law and raised marriage to a new dignity.

PART TWO

Chapter Five
Marriage in the New Testament

Monogamous in form (with, however, the possibility of divorce), personal values respected, the importance of mutual love recognized—the Jewish marriage institution, on the threshold of the New Testament, reflected its prototype with laudable fidelity; yet the coming of Christ was to transform it. Henceforth, the model of marriage is no longer the first, perfect marriage of man and woman but something infinitely more sublime: the supernatural union of Christ and his Church. It is to St. Paul we owe this doctrine, this vision. But the passage (Eph 5:22-33) which presents the archetype marks the climax of Christian teaching on marriage; before we can come to that we must consider what the rest of the New Testament has to say .

For the Sake of the Kingdom

Though it seems paradoxical we must, if we are to see it in proper perspective, preface our study of the New Testament doctrine of marriage by outlining the New Testament view on celibacy.[1] It is necessary to do so because marriage is an institution of this present world, while Christian life should always be marked by eschatological expectation, a looking to the future.[2] And in the world to come marriage will no longer exist. This is expressed very clearly in Lk 20:34-36: "The children of this age marry and are given in marriage. But they who are accounted worthy to attain to that world and to the resurrection from

---

1. The passage Apoc. 14:1-5 — the 144,000 companions of the Lamb described as 'virgins' does not belong in this context. The designation 'virgins' must be understood in a metaphorical sense. In view of the prophetical marriage image, idolatry on Israel's part was regarded as fornication or adultery. In Apoc. the 144,000 are contrasted with the followers of the Beast (13:3f,8,14-17) precisely because they have not adored the Beast but have remained faithful to the Lamb. They have remained virgins because they have not given themselves to the cult of the Beast but have clung to God; in the context there is no question of Christian ascetics. See M.-E. Boismard, "Notes sur l'Apocalypse", Revue Biblique, 59 (1952), pp. 161-172.

2. Eschatology (teaching concerning the end) is the hope of a divine intervention which brings about a radical change in the conditions of human life and in the relations between God and man. In the New Testament it is connected with the Parousia, the 'appearance' of Christ in divine power when, as ultimate savior and judge, he will come to complete his work. In the early Church eschatological tension, the vivid expectation of the Parousia, was a marked feature of Christian life.

the dead neither marry nor are given in marriage; for they cannot die any more, since they are equal to the angels, and are children of God, being children of the resurrection" (cf. Mk 12:25; Mt 22:30). In this world marriage is necessary for the continuation of the race. But in the next world those who have risen are, like the angels, immortal—there is no longer any need for marriage. Furthermore, the risen ('children of the resurrection' is a semitism) are children of God, sharing in God's life and glory and raised above earthly preoccupations. But in the person of Christ the Kingdom has come and those who have received the charism of religious celibacy have already, in a special but true sense, taken on this state of 'children of the resurrection.' They have turned from concern over this passing world to concern for the coming of the kindom in its fulness. And, at the same time, they have left themselves free to serve the Lord of the Kingdom.

* * *

This second factor, too, is part of the teaching of Jesus. In Mt. 19:3-9 he answered a query of the Pharisees by a blunt assertion that marriage is indissoluble. They objected that Moses, in the Law, had permitted divorce; he pointed out that this was because of their hardness of heart. Henceforth, in his kingdom and under the New Law, divorce would never be lawful (we will return to this point). We can gather that this teaching was not very favorably received by the Pharisees, but the disciples were also disconcerted. They said rather petulantly that if such were the case it would be better not to marry at all. They had visions of an unhappy marriage from which there would be no release. Jesus took up this grumble of the disciples and showed that abstention from marriage can be virtuous and may, indeed, be a special vocation. They had thought that it might be better for a man not to marry—for selfish reasons. Now they are taught that one may renounce marriage from a quite different motive. Jesus realized that what he said would not appeal to everybody, and he pointed out that not all would understand his teaching, but those only who were enlightened; not all would follow his counsel, but those only who were called. To the two classes of unmarriageable persons recognized by Judaism—'eunuchs by birth' and 'eunuchs by men'—he adds a third: 'eunuchs for the kingdom.' And his message is this: While there are some who for natural or other reasons cannot marry, there are others who freely renounce it 'for the sake of the kingdom of heaven' (19:12). But because the call is not addressed to all Christians (19:10), 'for the sake of the kingdom' must mean to leave oneself free for the preaching of the kingdom.

This voluntary renunciation of marriage was something new for Jews[3] They believed that all men were bound by the first blessing of the Law (which they interpreted as a command): "Be fruitful and multiply and fill the earth" (Gen 1:28). So it was that Christ anticipated the surprised reaction of his disciples by pointing out that a special vocation is involved. He stated: "Not all can receive (that is, understand and accept) this word, but only those to whom it is granted" (19:10) and he concluded: "He who is able to accept this, let him accept it" (19:21). Marriage is good, but there is a more perfect way. This way of life, however, is not mere abstention from marriage —this could well be for selfish reasons as the disciples had suggested. It is the motive that counts: renunciation must be made for the sake of the kingdom of God.

Paul on Virginity

Paul, in his turn, has to give his views on celibacy when he answers questions, submitted to him by his

---

3. According to Pliny and Josephus the Jewish sect of the Essenes abstained from marriage. However, it is not clear from the Dead Sea Scrolls that the sect of Qumran practiced celibacy, or, at least, perpetual celibacy.

Corinthian converts, on the matter of marriage and virginity (1 Cor 7). And though he does not seem to be aware of Christ's pronouncement (Mt 19:12)—since he puts forward not a decision of the Lord but his own opinion (1 Cor 7:25)—his teaching harmonizes with that of his Master. But he is at pains to show that though the celibate state is laudable—preferable even—yet marriage is a good thing too. He says that it is good to abstain from marriage but, because of danger of sin, it is often wiser to marry (7:1f). He goes on to speak of the duties of marriage and then adds: "I wish that all were as I myself am (that is, unmarried); but each receives his particular gift from God, some one thing and some another" (7:7). He realizes, as Jesus had indicated, that the state of virginity is not for everybody, that a special call of grace was needed for this way of life. Nevertheless, he repeats his advice: it is a good thing to remain unmarried (7:8).

Jesus had told us that the choice of a state of celibacy should be in view of the kingdom of God. Paul elaborates. He wants his Christians to be as free from worldly entanglements as possible. Now marriage can, and must to a certain extent, involve one in worldly matters: "The married man is concerned with worldly affairs, how to please his wife. . . . The married woman is concerned with worldly affairs, how to please her husband" (7:33f). This is the difficulty, and the danger, that Paul sees. Marriage is good, but it tends to become absorbing; a man or a woman may get quite lost in mundane matters. He is certainly not denying that, for married people, sanctification is to be sought and attained in and through family life, but he points out that family cares can be a distraction and may easily win one's whole attention. The contrast in these verses makes his meaning clear and also underlies the chief advantage that he sees in the unmarried state: "The unmarried man is concerned with the affairs of the Lord, how to please the Lord . . . the unmarried woman is concerned with the affairs of the Lord, that she may be holy in body and soul" (7:32, 34).

Thus, for Paul, the unmarried state is better than the married state because it leaves one free to serve the Lord. As he sees it, married people are torn between two allegiances (7:34); it is very difficult to give oneself wholeheartedly to the service of God when one is bound by family cares. Paul has been putting before his Corinthians an ideal. He insists on the dignity of marriage but he draws attention to and proposes another 'higher' state and he encourages those who are called to this charismatic state. And he concludes: "I tell you this in your own interest, not to lay any restraint upon you, but to direct you towards what is good, so that you may attend upon the Lord without distraction" (7:35).[4]

However, Paul's concern is not only that of unimpeded service of the Lord. He himself is a Christian of the first century. Thus we find that in 1 Thes 4:13-18, in view of his own vivid expectation of the second coming of his Lord, the Apostle has ranged himself among those who will be alive at that coming. Did he believe and does he teach that the Parousia is really near at hand? In the very next passage he admits that he does not know the date of the Parousia (5:1-3) and he urges the faithful to be vigilant and to live the Christian life to the full (5:6-11), just as he later castigates those who, thinking that the last hour was imminent, saw no further purpose in work (2 Thes 3:6-13). Hopeful expectation of the Lord's

---

4. "The meaning of I Cor. 7:36-38 is ambiguous. The man and the virgin of the passage are understood by some to be the virgin and her father, by others to be the virgin and her betrothed, and by others to be the virgin residing in the household of a man who has engaged himself to protect her virginity. In the first hypothesis it is supposed that the virgin has not her own decision concerning marriage, but is given in marriage by her father. The second hypothesis implies a recommendation of virginal espouses or even of virginal marriage. The third hypothesis postulates an early Christian practice which made it possible for young women to leave their father's house (and thus escape being given in marriage) and reside where they could preserve their virginity." J. L. McKenzie, **Dictionary of the Bible** (Milwaukee: Bruce, 1965), p. 914.

coming is one thing—and this expectation Paul shared with the early Christians—but a declaration that the Parousia was near at hand is another matter. This Paul never uttered. Yet the expectation is surely present in 1 Cor 7: 25-31 where it has given force to his counsel of virginity. In this perspective earthly things have lost their importance to the Christian.[5]

We have considered part of Paul's teaching in 1 Cor 7; it will be helpful to give an outline of the chapter before taking up what he has to say in it regarding

5. See R. Schnackenburg, **The Moral Teaching of the New Testament** (New York: Herder & Herder, 1965), pp. 189-191. E. Schillebeeckx writes: "The fundamental tendency in 1 Cor. 7 is Paul's stripping of marriage of the absolute value which it had in the Old Testament. Here he is not so much discussing celibacy as the newness of total abstinence which Christianity proposes as a possibility for every Christian, whatever his status in life may be. Anyone who denies that Paul, deeply concerned as he was for the kingdom of God, did not regard a life of complete abstinence as the ideal state is bound to do violence to these texts. It is, of course, indisputable that he came later (in Eph. 5) to a deeper insight into the christological significance of marriage itself and its meaning within the life of the Church, but this does not mean that his basic intuition of 1 Cor. 7 was swept aside. Whereas Genesis said that it was not good for man to be alone, Paul — astonishingly enough for a Jew — reached the point where he could state that it was indeed good for man to "be alone"! (see 7:25 f). — **Marriage: Secular Reality and Saving Mystery,** vol. I, Marriage in the Old and New Testaments. Translated by N. D. Smith (New York: Sheed & Ward, 1966), p. 188 f.

marriage. As we have seen, he favors the celibate state, but he acknowledges that marriage is good and he insists on the mutual conferring of conjugal rights (7:1-9). He reiterates the Lord's teaching concerning divorce (7:10f), but he gives his own view on mixed marriages (7:10-16). Then, by association of ideas, he turns to exhort Christians to remain in the way of life which the Lord has assigned to each (7:17-24) and follows this general admonition with further advice on virginity (7:25-38) and on widowhood (7:39f). The essential teaching of the whole section is: In principle one should remain in the state of life in which one found oneself on accepting the faith; virginity is a charismatic state with certain well-defined spiritual advantages; marriage is recommended to those who cannot otherwise resist concupiscence— it is a safeguard. One should turn to Eph 5:22-33 to get the Apostle's positive teaching on marriage.[6]

Paul on Marriage

Throughout 1 Cor 7 (and on to chapter 10) Paul answers questions raised in a letter of the Corinthian community to him. Corinth was at the time capital of the Roman province of Achaia and seat of the pro-

6. See E. Osty, **Les Epitres de Saint Paul aux Corinthiens** {BJ}, (Paris: Cerf, 1949), p. 38.

consul. Lying on the narrow isthmus, between the ports of Cenchreae in the east and Lechaeum in the west, it was a vital stage in traffic between West and East. Because of its position and commercial status it had an extremely varied population. Famous for its temple of Aphrodite on the summit of Acrocorinth— the steep hill above the city—it was, by the same token, a byword for sexual immorality (and that even in the world of Paul's day [cf Rom 1:26-32]) and the morals of the Christian converts, who themselves had come from and lived in that atmosphere, had to be built up without support from a natural morality. Against this background the questions of the Corinthian Christians on marriage and virginity have a particular poignancy which must be kept in mind when we evaluate Paul's replies.

Evidently the Corinthian attitude to marriage was uncertain. In reaction to the pagan licence there was a current which took a rigid attitude towards sexuality and regarded marriage as in some degree un-Christian. Paul states that celibacy in itself is a good thing (7:1; cf 7:25-35) but it is not for all, and one who is not called to virginity should marry (7:2).

A false or imprudent asceticism in regard to sexual intercourse can actually give Satan an opportunity to lead one into sin (7:5). And even if the Apostle does no more than offer prudent advice, and does not rule out continence (7:6), his words are a candid

and ungrudging acknowledgment of the essential goodness of normal marital relations. Despite his own obvious preference for celibacy (7:7) Paul, both as a Jew
and as a clear-sighted Christian, has a healthy appreciation of marriage. When he states that 'each one
has his own special gift (*charisma*) from God, one of
one kind and one of another' (7:7) he declares that
marriage is a 'charism,' a gift of God, just as much as
virginity. And if he does propose marriage as a remedy
for concupiscence ('it is better to marry than to be
aflame with passion' [7:9]), that is manifestly not the
whole of it. What the Apostle has to say about divorce
and mixed marriages will be considered below.

Paul put forward his main teaching on marriage
(apart from the notable development of Ephesians) in
the earliest of his epistles: "For this is the will of God
—your sanctification; that you keep yourselves from
impurity; that each of you should know how to take
a wife for himself in holiness and honor, not in the
passion of lust like the heathen who know not God"
(1 Thes 4:3-5). And towards the close of his life
he hit out at certain encratists[7] who 'forbid marriage'

---

7. The Encratites were groups of early Christians, mostly
of Gnostic bent, who abstained from wine, flesh-meat and
marriage, and carried their ascetic practice and doctrine to
extremes.

(1 Tim 4:3). An earlier text in the epistle seems to have the same situation in mind: "But woman will be saved through bearing children—if she continue in faith and love and holiness, together with modesty" (2:15). And in Tit 2:4f he exhorts the older woman to "train the young women to love their husbands and children, to be devout, chaste, domestic in their habits, kind, submissive to their husbands, that the word of God be not discredited."

Other Texts

From the admonition of Heb 13:4—"Let marriage be held in honor among all, and let the marriage bed be inviolate; for God will judge the immoral and adulterous"—it follows that marriage is an institution worthy of great respect and that husband and wife must observe the laws of marriage, especially chastity in marital relations (*koitē*, 'marriage bed' is a euphemism for sexual intercourse). *Amiantos* ('undefiled') is applied to the Temple in 2 Mac 14:36; 15:34 and characterizes the 'religion pure and undefiled' (Jas 1:27). We should preserve this cultic nuance: Christian spouses should be free from physical and moral stain, like their great immaculate High Priest (Heb 7:26). This is to say that unchastity would be both profanation and disloyalty. In his distinction of 'immoral' and 'adulterous' the author seems to have in mind not only adultery but also improper conduct within marriage.[8]

Peter too has something to say. In 1 Pet 3:1-7 wives are recommended to be subject to their husbands. Their attitude is all the more important in the case of an unbelieving husband (one who does not obey the word of the Gospel [cf 1:25]) who may be won by the conduct of his wife. Christian wives must not set store by external adornment (cf 1 Tim 2:9f) but in the interior beauty of a quiet and gentle spirit. They should look to the holy women of Israel: Sarah obeyed her husband and called him 'Lord' (Gen 18:12). By following her example they become the true children of Sarah. Christian husbands are admonished to treat their wives with great consideration and gentleness ('since they are the weaker sex') and to show them honor as co-heirs of the gift of eternal life; husband and wife are on terms of complete spiritual equality. The admonition to husbands closes with the words: 'that your prayers may not be hindered.' This seems to mean that 'where hardening of heart is caused by lack of understanding in the highest and most delicate of all human relationships, the relationship with God expressed in prayer is subject to serious

---

8. C. Spicq, L'Epitre aux Hébreux II, (Paris: Gabalda, 1953-, p. 418).

impediment. At the same time access to God in prayer is at once the goal and the test of human affection."[9]

Finally there is Apoc 19:7-9 which announces in joy and thanksgiving the day when the Messiah will celebrate his marriage with his people. Here (as in 2 Cor 11:2; Eph 5:25, 32) the prophetic image is taken over and transferred to the relationship of Christ and his Church (cf Apoc 21:2, 9; 22:17). The bride of the Lamb has prepared herself for the wedding; she has put on her wedding garments. Her wedding gown (that is her holiness) is a gift from God: it is the righteous deeds of the saints whom the bride represents. As in the Old Testament this imagery underlines the dignity of marriage.

Divorce

An essential aspect of New Testament teaching on marriage is the Lord's attitude to divorce. It is instructive to consider the circumstances of his formal pronouncement on the subject as the evangelists have recorded it (Mk 10:2:12; cf Mt 19:3-9). The Pharisees presented Jesus with a typical trick question: "Is it lawful to divorce one's wife on any grounds whatever?" (Mt 19:3). The question was patently framed

---

9. E. G. Selwyn, **The First Epistle of St. Peter** (London: Macmillan 1946), p. 188.

in the light of the Hillel-Shammai controversy; it was felt that he would have to come down on one side or the other and so give offence to one group. But he disconcerted his questioners as he had previously done to a fundamental principle which they had ignored. True enough, the controversialists had found a starting-point in the Law (cf Dt 24:1-4), which permitted divorce, but the legal provision was a concession to the hardness of men's hearts and had no part in the ideal of marriage as it had been instituted by God in the beginning; the ideal which Jesus now not only recalled but which he reiterated as a new and binding law:

> From the beginning of creation God 'made them male and female. For this reason a man shall leave his father and mother, and the two shall become one flesh.' So they are no longer two but one flesh only. What, therefore, God has joined together man must not part (Mk 10:6-9; cf Mt 19:4-6).

And in reply to a query of his disciples he put his absolute prohibition of divorce beyond question:

> Whoever divorces his wife and marries another commits adultery against his wife; and if she divorces her husband and marries another she commits adultery (Mk 10:11f; cf Lk 16:18).

It follows that not only does he regard marriage as an indissoluble union but that he has placed husband and wife in a relationship of equality. This unequivocal attitude colors the whole of New Testament teaching on marriage (cf in particular 1 Cor 7:10f). In the light of it the troublesome phrase of Mt 19:9; 5:32 cannot countenance divorce—whatever else it may mean.

The saying on divorce is one of the many doublets of Matthew's Gospel: the evangelist not only has it in the same context as Mark, but he also includes it in his synthesis of the Lord's teaching that we know as the Sermon on the Mount. In both places he adds the clause 'except for *porneia*.'[10] We may reasonably take it that the phrase was added by the evangelist himself; it is not the only time he has made such additions. Writing as he is for Jewish readers, *porneia* has for him the same meaning that it has in Acts 15:20, 29 and refers to marriage within the degrees of kinship prohibition by Jewish law. Matthew wants to make it clear that Jesus was not referring to such 'marriages,' which were already null and void. We might paraphrase his text like this: "If anyone divorces his wife he may not marry again, except when his mar-

10. **Porneia** is usually rendered 'fornication' its meaning is wider, and can reasonably include marriage within the forbidden degrees (Lev. 18:6-18).

riage was not a real one at all, but had only the appearance of one."[11]

Paul reiterated the Lord's prohibition of divorce: "To the married I command—indeed not I but the Lord—that the wife shall not separate from her husband (but even if she does separate let her remain unmarried, or else be reconciled to her husband), and that the husband shall not divorce his wife" (7:10f); and he repeats it later on: "A wife is bound to her husband as long as he lives" (7:39; cf Rom 7:2f). It seems that 1 Cor 7:15 must be understood in the light of these declarations: "If [in a mixed marriage] the unbelieving partner agrees to separate, let him or her do so; in such case the believing brother or sister is not slavishly bound (*ou dedoulōtai*)" that is, he or she is not obliged to strive to maintain or re-establish the marriage at any price. Paul does not seem to envisage the possibility of another marriage; that is made possible only by death (7:39; Rom 7:1-3). Generally in the past, and to some extent today, exegesis has seen the 'Pauline privilege' expressed in this text, and the phrase 'not slavishly bound' is taken to refer to the marriage bond. Against this interpretation it may be observed that the Apostle in 1 Cor 7:39 and Rom

---

11. H. J. Richards, "Christ on Divorce", **Scripture**, 11 (1959), p. 30. The solution here indicated is admirably presented in the article cited, pp. 22-32.

7:2, where he does undoubtedly refer to the marriage bond, uses the verb *deō*, 'to bind.'[12]

Paul's view of a mixed marriage (for him, a marriage between a Christian and a pagan) is that if the pagan partner, the 'unbeliever,' consents to live with

---

12. See J. B. Bauer, **Bibeltheologisches Worterbuch** (Graz/ Wien/Koln: Styria, 1962²), p. 210. "The so-called Pauline privilege which has found a place in Canon Law (C.I.C. 1120-1124, 1126), and is there strictly delimited, is based on 1 Cor. 7:15 ff. When in a purely pagan marriage one partner accepts the Christian faith and the other is not willing to continue the marriage, the Christian party is free to contract a new marriage. According to the context, of course, Paul is only dealing with the question whether separation is permissible in such a case; he does not speak of remarriage. Nor can the right to remarry be inferred from **ou dedoulotai.** However verses 15c to 16 are interpreted, whether as intended to console the Christian party (taking verse 16, therefore, in the sense of "leave them in the care of God"), or as an exhortation rather to continue the marriage because perhaps the conversion of the pagan partner may still be possible after all (this was the view of John Chrysostom and Thomas Aquinas and one that has found favor again today), there is no mention of remarriage. The general tendency of the passage (cf. verses 10 ff) would not seem to point in that direction either, especially if the interpretation we have just mentioned were accepted. The Pauline privilege, therefore, is an extension of the Pauline concession of separation, developed by the Church's teaching authority in favor of the believing partner. For the Church's decision in this, however, the point is of importance that the Christian partner in such a case is abandoning a natural marriage in order to contract a Christian, sacramental marriage." R. Schnackenburg, op. cit., p. 249 f.

the Christian partner the latter should not separate. Since both are one flesh the sanctification of the one reaches to the other; that is, the whole home benefits from the fact that the Spirit of God dwells in one of the partners. In other words, since Christian marriage is a special gift, a charism from God (7:7), it is even in a mixed marriage a sanctifying force: "For the unbelieving husband is sanctified through his wife and the unbelieving wife is sanctified through her husband" (7:14). A remark of the Apostle suggests that the children of such a marriage were regarded as 'saints,' that is as Christians (7:14).[13] If we take 7:16 as the conclusion of the whole passage and not just as following from the preceding verse, then it seems that, trusting in the sanctifying power of marriage, Paul recommends the maintenance of the marriage union with the unconverted partner.

The Status of Women

In the first century A.D. the social status of women in Jewish society was not high; we have seen that they had few rights in law. The teaching of Jesus did not seek to change the situation in any radical way

---

13. See H. Cazelles, "Marriage, Dans le Nouveau Testament", **DBS**, V, c. 929.

but his own attitude toward women was of decisive significance. And the sensitive Luke, more than the other evangelists, noted the courtesy of Christ. Among the women introduced in his Gospel are the widow of Naim (17:11-17), the repentant sinner (7:36-50), the women of Galilee who accompanied Jesus on the public ministry, notably Mary Magdalen, Joanna and Susanna (8:2f) who were with him at the end (23:55f), the sisters of Bethany, Martha and Mary (10:38-42). There are also the woman who declared the mother of Jesus blessed (11:27f), and the women of Jerusalem who met Jesus on his way to Calvary (23:27-31). We find besides two parables proper to Luke in which women figure: The Lost Coin (15:8-10) and The Unjust Judge (18:1-8). And it is impossible not to recognize that the person of Mary is shown in a vivid light in the Infancy narrative. John also noted Jesus' friendship with the family of Bethany ("Now Jesus loved Martha and her sister and Lazarus" [11:5]) and remarked how his conversation with the lone woman at Jacob's well had rather shocked the strait-laced conventional view of his disciples (4:27).

It is surely this example of the Master which assured that women played an important role in the apostolic Church. Women were present in the Cenacle (Acts 1:14, 26) and took part in the election of Matthias (cf 1:15) and presumably received the Spirit at Pentecost (2:1-4). They received the charisms (21:9) and could 'prophesy' in the liturgical assembly (1 Cor 11:5). Many women were in the service of the Gospel (cf 1 Cor 1:11; Phil 4:2; Rom 16:1, 6, 12, 15; Col 4:15). We find one at least, Priscilla, giving instruction in the faith (Acts 18:26). Widows, or a special class of widows, had official standing and rendered special service in the churches (1 Tim 5:9-15). All this was alien to the Jewish spirit and also went far beyond the accepted views of the hellenistic world on the position of women in society.

Yet a number of texts of Paul would seem to indicate that he, for one, had not developed far beyond the social horizon of the Old Testament in this matter. It is particularly noteworthy that he several times calls the husband the 'head' of the wife (1 Cor 11:3, 5; Eph 5:23) and requires obedience of the wife (Col 3:18; Eph 5:22, 24; Tit 2:5; cf 1 Pet 3:1-7). The first thing to observe is that these references almost always occur in 'social' or 'household codes.'[14] These simply reflect the social structures of the environment

14. A means of ethical instruction well known in antiquity was the social code; Old Testament examples are Tob chs. 4 and 12; Sir. 7:18-35. In the New Testament 1 Pet. 2:13-3:12 follows closely the pattern of such a social or household code and finds close parallels in Col. 3:18-4:1; Eph. 5:22-6:9; 1 Tim. 2:8-15; 5:3-8; 6:1f; Tit 2:1-10. The method was current in the hellenistic world.

in which they were formulated. In large measure, the New Testament household codes echo those of the hellenistic world which were ethically sound; the essential difference, affecting the spirit rather than the latter, is that Christians must order their lives—in keeping with these ethical norms—'in the Lord,' that is, precisely as Christians.

The question arises, then, whether existing ethical forms are simply taken over, with no intention of turning them into unchangeable norms. And if this is the case, as it seems to be, we may admit that the assertion that the husband is 'head of the wife,' with the wife's consequent subordinate position and inferior social status, is conditioned by the social circumstances of the time. In view of the changed outlook on women in the modern world and the new social position which she occupies not only in the family but in public life it does seem that biblical assertions about women must be judged in their own setting, and re-evaluated in the light of the present social setting. "In a nutshell, the problem is this: Is the statement, 'the husband is the head of the wife,' an authentically biblical assertion, based on revelation, which was of course bound to be experienced in accordance with and within existing social structures? Or is it a biblical assertion at all, but merely something taken over from the ancient idea of *paterfamilias* [that is, the almost absolute rights of a man over his family—wife and children] and expressed in Christian terms?"[15]

In referring to the husband as 'head of the woman' Paul has the Genesis creation narratives in view. And he regards the Yahwistic account (first man is created, then woman) as setting the pattern for the actual social status of woman. In 1 Tim 2:13 he says: "Adam was made first, then Eve." For him it is not only a matter of chronology but an arrangement of nature: man has a leading function and woman a subordinate function. So even while he appeals to the Genesis account he is obviously being influenced by the social situation which he knew and in which woman occupied a subordinate position.

His embarrassment is evident in 1 Cor 11:2-16 when he argues that the subordinate place of women in Christian liturgical assemblies is founded on the order of creation. His Jewish taste had been offended by the fact that Christian women of Corinth were praying and prophesying in public worship with heads uncovered. Perhaps he feared for their reputations since pagan temple prostitutes worshipped with heads uncovered. However, the arguments which he adduces are weak; he recognizes this himself in v. 16 and falls back on an appeal to the custom of the churches. But

---

15. E. Schillebeeckx, op. cit., p. 250. For a thorough discussion of the problem see ibid., pp. 243-282.

he emphatically asserts in this passage his own belief that man is the head of the woman. So we are still faced with the question: Is the doctrine (that the man is head of the wife who is therefore subject to her husband) a biblical *datum*? Or is it only a biblical *mode of thought and expression* and as such open to modification in changed social and historical circumstances? To this question Edward Schillebeeckx has given a finely nuanced reply:

> We may therefore conclude that what is involved in Paul's assertion, 'the husband is the head of the wife,' is an experience 'in the Lord' of an existing pattern of society and of family life, in which an absolute—though historically conditioned—datum of 'natural law' may be implied. Moreover, Paul's tendency to provide these hierarchical structures which were already present in society with a 'theological' basis, and thus to give them an independent value, is clearly expressed in this assertion, with the result that we get the impression that we are dealing here with a constant and unchangeable structure bestowed on marriage by God himself. In the New Testament there is yet no explicit recognition that revelation does not exclude the growth of human awareness, or the development of the historical significance of the values in this and similar spheres of life which

have, in the first instance, a secular and existential significance.[16]

At any rate it is evident that the answer to our question is not so obvious as a superficial reading of the texts might suggest.

Very important here is a certain tension in Paul's appreciation of woman's status. His declaration in Gal 3:28 that in Christ 'there is neither slave nor free, there is neither man nor woman, but all are one,' is a clear statement of the dignity of woman: precisely as a Christian she is nowise inferior to man. In the matter of the conjugal rights and duties of husband and wife he took his stand on the principle of perfect equality (1 Cor 7:3f, 12). Even in 1 Cor 11 he modified his contention that the husband was the head of the wife (11:8f) by immediately adding: "Nevertheless, in the Lord, woman is not independent of man nor man of woman; for as woman was taken from man, so man is now born of woman" (11:11f). Peter (1 Pet 3:1-7) ends on the same note: The husband should be considerate towards his wife and show her honor because they are 'equal inheritors of the gift of life.' Hence whatever the actual inequality of man and woman in society, both sexes enjoy equal dignity 'in the Lord.'

16. Ibid., p. 277.

And when we consider that in fact, as we have observed, the status of women in the Christian communities quickly outgrew Jewish and hellenistic convention, we will realize that Paul's assertions (like those of Peter) on the subjection of woman to man are not only the reflection of their own Jewish formation but are matters of hierarchical and pastoral guidance, in a definite historical setting. "The theological lesson to be drawn from this is that having established that this is basically a question of a variable social and historical factor does not in fact clear the matter up once and for all—there still remains the question of the church's conduct in pastoral affairs, and the question of personal decision on grounds of individual conscience."[17]

In conclusion and by way of a summary we may observe that, in the New Testament, marriage is seen as a fact of creation which has won a new dignity within the Christian order of things. The essential goodness of marriage in all its aspects is stressed; it is made quite clear for instance that mutual sexual obligations may not be neglected for ascetic reasons. At the same time, however, marriage has lost the absolute value which it had in the Old Testament, and

17. Ibid., p. 281 f.

celibacy, as a vocation, is seen as a response to the eschatological tension within Christianity. From the personal point of view, marriage is a lifelong commitment and constitutes an indissoluble union. It must be so since Christian marriage reflects the loving union of Christ and his Church.

Chapter Six

The Great Mystery

At the start of the previous chapter we observed that Eph. 5:22-33 marks the climax of New Testament teaching on marriage. Now we are in a position to study this passage which brings forth as the model of marriage the union of Christ and his Church. Undoubtedly there is already a preparation for the Pauline concept in the prophetical theme of the marriage of Yahweh and Israel but it is nonetheless significant that the Apostle, in elaborating his teaching, does not refer at all to the Old Testament image. His doctrine, though quite in harmony with the older idea, is essentially something new. Perhaps we have said all that can be said when we assert that Paul has shown us the meaning of *Christian* marriage.

In his epistle to the Colossians St. Paul has, among a series of exhortations on family and social obligations, a few words of practical advice for husbands and wives:

Wives, be subject to your husbands, as is fitting in the Lord.

Husbands, love your wives and do not be harsh with them (3:18-19). Then, in Ephesians—that finest synthesis of his thought which was written shortly after Colossians and along the same lines, but in a much more tranquil frame of mind—he takes up the same theme. Now, however, from practical advice it is transformed into theology, the theology of Christian marriage.

The text of Ephesians 5:21-33 is the beginning of a long passage devoted to family relations—it is a household code—quite like Colossians. The opening verse is a general exhortation: "Be subject to one another out of reverence for Christ" (5:21) and the following verse is almost the same as in the earlier epistle: "Wives, look to your husbands as to the Lord" (5:22; cf Col 3:18). But at this point, in Ephesians, a striking motive is added:

> For the husband is head of his wife just as Christ is head of the Church, he the Savior of the Body. But just as the Church is subject to Christ so must wives be subject to their husbands in everything (5:23f).

The Body of Christ

Here we encounter the distinctive Pauline doctrine of the Body of Christ and this we must consider first of all. When in 1 Cor 12:12 Paul states that Christians form one body he is not speaking metaphorically and is not referring to a Greek fable of the body and its members (12:14-26). It is the personal body of Christ which draws together the many members of the body which believers have become through baptism (12:13, 27) and by eucharistic communion (10:17). Around the individual body of Jesus the unity of men, called to join themselves to this body, is achieved.[1]

The highest point reached by 1 Cor on the theme of the body of Christ is found in 12:12f, 27: "For just as the body is one, yet has many members, and all the members of the body, though many, are yet one body. . . . Now you are the body of Christ, and individually members of it." At this point in Paul's thought *sōma* ('body') meant the physical body of Christ; it is the real body of Christ present in the Eucharist. (Indeed, the expression 'mystical body of Christ,' now applied to the Church, originally designated the eucharistic body of the Lord). Union with

1. See F. Amiot, **Vocabulaire de Théologie Biblique** (Ed. X. Léon-Dufour) (Paris: Cerf, 1962), p. 166.

the body of Christ means union with the eucharistic body, or the union which comes about through baptism into Christ. Though Paul was influenced by the hellenistic figure of the body and its members as representative of the social order there is yet no concept of the body of Christ in the sense of the Church as it will appear in the captivity epistles.[2]

Colossians, with its cosmic view of the heavenly Christ, clearly distinguishes the Church from him who is its Head (cf Col 1:18, 24). Its character of 'Body of Christ,' which was already met with in the earlier epistles, takes on a fresh relief and a stronger realism. The Church is the Body of Christ because it is made up of all Christians whose bodies are joined by baptism to the physical body of the risen Christ and receive from him the new life of the Spirit.

The gathering together of the saved is made 'in one Man' (Eph 2:15) who is Christ, prototype of the new humanity, 'in one Body' (2:16) which is his body, crucified and dead to sin, and 'in one Spirit' (2:12) which is the Spirit of the risen Lord. Here we have the theme of the Body of Christ at its most profound. And here less than ever can it be a metaphorical application of the profane image of the 'social

2. See L. Cerfaux **The Church in the Theology of St. Paul.** Translated by G. Webb and A. Walker, (New York: Herder & Herder, 1959), pp. 266-282.

body.' It is something very different: the expansion of the individual body of Christ, dead and risen, by the joining to it, through baptism, of the bodies of Christians; and so it reaches out to the dimensions of the great Body of the Church. And at the same time a distinction is maintained between the Body which is built up on earth and the Head which directs its growth from heaven (Eph 4:15f; cf Col 2:19). The whole structure of the Church is founded on unity and leads to unity (Eph 4:1-16). Finally Paul has brought out even more clearly the distinction of Head and Body (seen in the relationship of one to the other) and their union (achieved through love) when he represents the Church as the Spouse of Christ (5:23-32).[3]

The Archetype

In short it follows that all Christians together form the Body which Christ has saved and the Church which he has baptized (5:23, 26). As the Body of Christ the Church is intimately attached to him; yet he as Head remains distinct and the Church is subject to him in loving obedience, thus providing the pattern

3. See P. Benoit, **Les Epitres de Saint Paul aux Philippiens, à Philémon, aux Colossiens, aux Ephèsiens (BJ)**, (Paris: Cerf. 1959³), pp. 52 f, 78-80.

of the obedience which every wife owes to her husband.[4] For Paul has realized that the marriage image most forcibly expresses the intimate union of Christ and his Church. So he has set up a parallel between the husband-wife relationship and the union of Christ and his Church: husband and wife, in their marriage, verify this union and make it manifest by their personal relations. The Christ-Church relationship is thus the archetype of Christian marriage and it is precisely in view of the archetype (he explains) that the wife must be subject to her husband in all things.[5] Of

4. E. Schillebeeckx, op. cit., p. 272: "The chief function of the man is not somehow **inferred** from the mystery of Christ as a kind of conclusion here; what Paul does is to associate the **already existing and generally accepted** position of the man as head with Christ — and there is all the difference in the world between the two. Moreover, it is already clear in 1 Cor. 11 that this function of the man was not a theological fact, but a situation that was already present in society to which Paul gave a theological superstructure."

5. Ibid. p. 276: "The relationship between Christ and his Church was made present in a special way in Christian marriage, but the idea of head and subjection, which is real in the case of the relationship between Christ and the Church, was in marriage only a fact determined by social and historical conditions. Paul was able to combine the two aspects of the one image, but from the exegetical and theological point of view it is by no means evident that the man was established as head of the family **by revealed truth,** or that revealed truth confirmed a natural law to the effect that the husband is head of the wife."

course the human couple cannot measure up to the divine model and already the essential difference is manifest: Christ is the *Savior* of the Church.[6]

The Apostle then turns to husbands, urging them to love their wives, and again adds the reason for that love:

> Husbands, love your wives, as Christ loved the Church: he gave himself up for her, that he might sanctify her, having cleansed her in the laver of water with the word, so that he might present the Church to himself all glorious, without spot or wrinkle or any such thing, but holy and immaculate (5:25-27).

The statement that wives must be subject to their husbands may, at first—and especially to modern ears—strike a disturbing note (see our treatment of the problem in the preceding chapter), but the example of the Church's subjection to Christ, and the reference to him as Savior, should clearly set the recommendation in proper perspective. More forcibly, the parallel exhortation to husbands makes it patent that there is nothing humiliating about such subjection, for husbands are exhorted to love their wives, not in any fashion, but after the manner of Christ. And Christ

6. See H. Schlier, **Der Brief an die Epheser** (Düsseldorf: Patmos, 1962²), p. 253.

loved the Church and gave himself up for her that he might sanctify her; he purified her by washing her clean of every stain in the nuptial bath of baptism and presented her to himself as his spotless bride. Against this background the subjection of the wife—a loving subjection, needless to say—is offset, and even quite outweighed, by the love of her husband.

St. Paul next passes to a new thought, one that sprang to mind when he recalled the text of Gen 2:24. It suggests to him another reason why husbands ought to love their wives:

> In the same way, husbands should love their wives as their own bodies. In loving his wife a man loves himself. For no man ever hated his own flesh; on the contrary he nourishes and cherishes it. And that is how Christ treats the Church —for we are members of his Body. "For this reason a man shall leave his father and mother and be joined to his wife, and the two shall become one single flesh" (5:28-31).

It is obviously a truism that a man will look after his own body. But according to the text of Genesis, which establishes the divine institution of marriage, man and wife form one single being; therefore in loving his wife a man is only loving himself. This argument, admittedly banal, is lifted to a new level by the further observation that Christ, too, nourishes and cherishes his Church, which is his Body as it is his Bride. Nor is this Paul's last word for he adds, again with reference to the Genesis text: "This mystery is great— I take it to mean Christ and the Church" (5:32).

The argument of the Apostle in the passage 5:28-32 comes to this:[7] Husbands should love their wives as they love their own bodies. Everyone loves his own flesh; so also Christ loves the Church, his Body. This is the meaning of Gen 2:24 when one sees there a type of Christ and the Church. For Paul has in mind not the marriage relationship in general but the human prototype of marriage, that of Adam and Eve; and Adam, who cleaves to his wife, is in his view a type of Christ who loves his Church. That is precisely the great mystery of which he speaks—great not because of its mysteriousness but because of its significance and sublimity. Adam and Eve, precisely in their relationship of husband and wife—for that is the sense of Gen 2:24—are types of Christ and his Church. And in the measure in which each earthly marriage of man and woman reflects the mystery of the marriage of Christ and his Church, it shares in that mystery. Here, in one breath, are associated the archetype and prototype of marriage and the marriages in which the ideal is more or less realized. It is obvious that only Christian marriage (when it is

7. Ibid., p. 262.

truly such) can hope to reproduce with any fidelity the perfect lines of the archetype.

Coming after this, the last verse might sound like an anti-climax; instead it strikingly brings out the essentially practical nature of Christianity. Christians may have their eyes raised to heaven but they must strive to give flesh and bone to sublime ideals in a world that is the home of men and not of angels. So the parting admonition of the Apostle, immediately after he has conjured up the divine archetype, is not banal but shows a spirit of realism and an appreciation of actual conditions that forcibly set off the foregoing teaching.

However, for your part, let each one of you love your wife as himself, and let the wife see that she reveres her husband (5:33). Once again, as at the beginning, love is recommended to the husband and reverence to the wife. For on both of these, on love and on reverence mutually expressed, is marriage founded and by means of these it reflects the prototype already sketched in Gen 2:24, that mysterious image of the marriage of Christ and his Church.

It is, however, in heaven that the marriage-feast of Christ is celebrated because only there will his Church appear glorious and without blemish "as a Bride adorned for her husband" (Apoc 21:2; cf. 19:7f). Before she can come to that she has to be purified by him, cleansed of every stain; it is still the time of purification but she knows that she is his chosen one. But the Church is no vague personification, it is a living organism made up of men and women, of beings who are not only human but fallen and whose fallen state is evident, among other ways, in the rebellion of their sex instincts. Yet, it is before such men and women that Scripture has set a standard which was progressively raised to match the development of revelation; monogamous marriage, the marriage-image of Yahweh and Israel, the marriage-type of Christ and his Church. It is to the ultimate ideal that Christian husbands and wives must lift their gaze and must seek to reproduce in their lives the lines of that perfect union. It is by sanctifying their married life that they can win for themselves a place at the 'marriage supper of the Lamb' (Apoc 19:9) when they, husbands and wives, with all the elect, will be, not guests, but, all together, the spotless Bride of Christ.

This lofty ideal of marriage is certainly not meant to discourage Christians. True enough, the ideal is altogether beyond the unaided efforts of flesh and blood, but Christ offers his help in the sacrament he has instituted. And Paul, who outlined the ultimate doctrine of marriage, was very well aware of the actual condition of men and women. He realized that Christians have not been restored to the state of integrity, that they must still struggle against all the sinful tendencies of a fallen nature. In sexual matters there is the danger of disorders quite opposed to Christian holiness. Christian liberty is not license; the body of a baptized person belongs to the Lord as a member of his, so that sexual union outside of marriage is a monstrous parody of the divine plan (1 Cor 6:12-20). "This false union, founded on passion alone, degrades and profanes the Temple of the Holy Spirit which we are; on the other hand, the true union, within the Christian scheme of things, has place for the flesh too, and that without turning the back on holiness."[8]

8. P. Grelot, op. cit. p. 78. E. Schillebeeckx, op. cit., pp. 284-286: "In connection with the rejection of prostitution in the New Testament, there is a passage in Paul which shows clearly how the author had an anthropological view of marital relationships — the becoming one of marriage — and at the same time provided a Christological background for this: 1 Cor. 6:12-20. This passage ought to be an inspiration to us in our dogmatic consideration of the whole question of marriage in Paul. The Apostle recognized that the Christian is closely bound to the glorified Christ even in his physical being. To emphasize this Paul refers to the resurrection in which our bodies will reflect the glory of Christ's spiritual body, and this destiny is already in a sense present for our bodies by virtue of baptism. Belonging to the body of the Lord, the Christian's own body is, so to speak, the body of Christ, so that he no longer has control of it, to use it against the will of Christ. Intercourse in marriage is a becoming one flesh. Association with a harlot is an offence against the one spirit which

Christian marriage demands life-long fidelity because, once again, it is modelled on the perfect union of Christ and his Church. But at the same time Christian husbands and wives share a human nature that is wounded and weak. They may feel the remorse of moral lapses; they may be faced with problems that seem well-nigh insoluble (we have only to think of the problem of family planning and its implication for Christians). In short, they will feel that though their sexual life has been sanctified in principle, by the sacrament, there still remains a struggle for self-mastery.

The relations of husband and wife have been trou-

the Christian has become with Christ. The one flesh which the Christian forms with Christ in belonging to his body, the Church, is here seen to be 'one spirit,' not in the later, 'ghostly' sense of 'spiritual', but in the original New Testament sense — the baptized Christian forms a **living community** with Christ. Paul is not seeking to establish a connection here between the 'one flesh' which baptized partners in marriage form and the 'one spirit' of the marriage covenant of the believer with Christ. All that he does is to contrast fornication with the living community with Christ. These are mutually exclusive, and Paul expresses that fact by contrasting one 'flesh' and 'one spirit'. There is, as Eph. v:22-32 so clearly shows, no contrast between the 'one flesh' of married Christians and the 'one spirit' which the believer forms with Christ. This idea is a very rewarding one from the dogmatic point of view; and from the anthropological point of view, the text implies that the sex act is not a superficial one, in which the person remains outside — on the contrary, the person in deeply involved."

bled by the Fall (Gen 3:6) and the perfect harmony intended by the Creator has been disrupted. Yet in the sacrament of matrimony they are offered the means to win back the unity that has been disturbed. Gradually, their mutual love, *in Christ*, will conquer their innate selfishness and will overcome the tensions of a sinful nature, for charity will entirely displace desire. But the victory will be won only at the price of daily fidelity to the redeeming grace of Christ.[9]

9. P. Grelot, op. cit., p. 95 f.

Chapter Seven
The Sacrament[1]

In the new creation, the new life in Christ, marriage has become a sacrament. Now a sacrament is a personal act of the glorified Christ who in and by visible action makes us participants in the mystery of his redemption, that is, in the mystery of Easter and Pentecost.[2] The grace proper to each sacrament is a

---

1. In this final chapter (which goes beyond the explicit data of Scripture and is, rather, in the fashion of an epilogue) I am content to summarize and paraphase some pages of a short but illuminating study of E. Schillebeeckx: Le Mariage est un Sacrament, (Brussels: La Pensée Catholique, 1961), pp. 19-22, 33-46.

2. "In the Resurrection, as the eternally-enduring act of salvation, there is also included Christ's ascension (cf. Jn. 20:17,21-23) and establishment as Lord (cf. Ac. 2:36; Rm. 1:4), the sending of the Holy Spirit which is Christ's actual exercise of lordship, and to a certain extent the parousia as well. In their essential core all these together form the single enduring mystery of salvation: the person of the humiliated and glorified Christ who is the saving reality." E. Schillebeeckx, Christ the Sacrament of Encounter with God, (New York: Sheed & Ward, 1963), p. 25.

specific participation in the mystery of Christ seen under a determined aspect in each case. Set organically in the ensemble of the sacraments of the Church, marriage has its own special significance; in it the spouses are introduced in a particular and original manner into the mystery of salvation, for they participate in the mystery precisely as husband and wife. Marriage is a participation in the mystery of redemption seen as the union of Christ with his beloved Church which he has won for himself as a holy bride. Those who marry 'in the Lord,' that is as baptized believers, share in a special manner, befitting their new situation as Christians, in the bond which makes of Christ and the Church 'one body.'[3]

Communion with the Lord

As a baptized person the believer belongs to the

3. "Christ the Lord abundantly blessed this many-faceted love, welling up as it does from the fountain of divine love and structured as it is on the model of his union with his Church. For as God of old made himself present to his people through a covenant of love and fidelity, so now the Savior of men and the Spouse of the Church comes into the lives of married Christians through the sacrament of matrimony. He abides with them thereafter so that as he loved the Church and handed himself over on her behalf, the spouses may love each other with perpetual fidelity through mutual self-bestowal." Vatican Council II: **Pastoral Constitution on the Church in the Modern World,** Part II, Ch. I, par. 48.

Church. It follows that, by baptism, he has already entered into the conjugal relationship that unites Christ and his Church. This intimate union—this communion of grace—reaches to the bodies of the baptized: "the body is for the Lord and the Lord for the body" (1 Cor 6:13): our bodies are members of the body of Christ (1 Cor 6:15; Eph 5:30-32). Thus a conjugal relationship to Christ the Lord already characterizes all Christian life. The marriage of two baptized persons is only a particular manifestation of this relationship but so distinctive is it that, in God's design, it merits a special sacrament.

For Christian spouses the fact of marriage means that the conjugal relationship which already unites each Christian to Christ now operates through their own marriage: it is in their specific relationship of reciprocal belonging that they belong to Christ. The community of love of married people becomes a form of communion with the Lord. All this follows from the fact that by baptism the believer has been radically consecrated, soul and body, to Christ; and now it is Christ alone who can give him to another being and bring it about that the spouses—as the nature of marriage demands—belong really and perfectly to each other. It is by means of, and within, their conjugal relationship, that communion of grace, that Christ himself gives two beings, man and woman, to each other.

Sanctifying Love

Though as a sacrament it is a means of sanctification, marriage is not so much the consecration of persons as the consecration of the *bond* which unites them: it is the consecration of an inter-personal relationship. And it is through this sanctified and sanctifying relationship that the persons themselves are sanctified. Now the proper bond of interpersonal relations is *love* and it follows that, by the sacrament of marriage, human conjugal love becomes a consecrated love, a religious reality.

Marriage is a visible sign of the love union of Christ and his Church and the saving love of Christ is present as a gift, a grace, in marriage. Conjugal life itself thereby becomes a means of sanctification.[4] Hus-

---

4. "Authentic married love is caught up into divine love and is governed and enriched by Christ's redeeming power and the saving activity of the Church, so that this love may lead the spouses to God with powerful effect and may aid and strengthen them in the sublime office of being a father or a mother. For this reason Christian spouses have a special sacrament by which they are fortified and receive a kind of consecration in the duties and dignity of their state. By virtue of this sacrament, as spouses fulfill their conjugal and family obligations, they are penetrated with the Spirit of Christ, which suffuses their whole lives with faith, hope and charity. Thus they increasingly advance the perfection of their own personalities, as well as their mutual sanctification, and hence contribute jointly to the glory of God." Ibid.

band and wife sanctify each other as Christ has sanctified the Church.[5] We may even say that from this point of view Christ's sanctification of the Church is by means of the conjugal relation of the spouses; because in them and by them, humanity, in the course of time, is truly sanctified. And in view of that supernatural union of love which it reflects, marriage is not only a sign of God's love for man, it is also a sign of man's love for God—in Christ. For in Christ and his Church God's love and man's response meet. Hence marriage should be marked by mutual love and response.

Marriage is a sacrament not in its starting-point only; the whole of married life is placed under the blessing of sacramental grace. Since as a sacrament this life is now a participation in the love of Christ and of his Church, the grace of marriage becomes active in and through the mutual love of husband and wife. It is not the family as such but the married state that is a sacrament. And so it is on the basis of conjugal love that Christian marriage must be lived and it is in the light of this love that we may appreciate the further blessing of marriage. The love of *father*

5. Though husband and wife, in their marriage, reflect, respectively, Christ and the Church yet, from another point of view, as members of the Body of Christ (the Church), wife and husband are both sanctified by Christ and, as members of his Body, interact one on the other.

for *mother* and mother for father is another form of that authentic love of man for woman and develops within this love. So sacramental grace penetrates the conjugal love which finds its term in procreation and so illuminates family love. And thus, from the central cell, the grace of marriage reaches out to the whole human community.

The Ministers

Because a sacrament is a personal act of Christ,[6] the principal minister of marriage is the Lord himself. This means that the conjugal link, as a sacrament, is a personal act, a manifestation of the love of Christ, who gives a woman to a man and a man to a woman; the mutual gift of self and acceptance of the other on the part of the spouses is the sacramental sign of the grace of Christ. It follows that bridegroom and bride are each, the one for the other, minister of the sacrament and, reciprocally, each receives it from the other;

6. "A sacrament is primarily and fundamentally a personal act of Christ himself, which reaches and involves us in the form of an institutional act performed by a person in the Church who, in virtue of the sacramental character, is empowered to do so by Christ himself." E. Schillebeeckx, Christ the Sacrament of the Encounter with God, p. 62.

to marry is an act of the priesthood of the baptized.[7]
As minister each gives himself or herself to the other
as a grace and represents for the other the love of
Christ for his Church. In so far as he or she receives
the sacrament each receives from the other, as a grace,
and realizes for the other the attitude of the Church
receiving grace in faith and love.

Sign of Redemption

Like all sacramental grace the grace of marriage
is also a grace of redemption: the beauty of conjugal
fidelity is manifested in fallen man only at the cost of
many sacrifices. So this sacrament is also an invitation
to enter into the mystery of the cross. By a love faithful unto death Christ acquired the Church for himself
as his faithful spouse and, after this model, the gift
of married love involves a real sharing in the cross.
It is not of course the sacrament itself which brings
about suffering and unhappiness in marriage, but the
hard facts of life: marriage difficulties, family troubles.
All kinds of bitter realities deeply set into the social

---

7. "The laity (therefore all Christians) share in the priestly,
prophetic and royal office of Christ. . . . They are consecrated
(by baptism) for the royal priesthood and the holy people (cf.
1 Pet. 2:4-10)." Vatican Council II, **Decree on the Apostolate
of the Laity,** Ch. I, par. 2,3.

reality of our sinful humanity—are introduced by the sacrament into the shadow of the cross—or rather into the light and the power of the crucified love of Christ. St. Thomas has said: "If marriage does not conform us to the suffering of Christ insofar as this is a penalty (that is, accepted as expiation for our sins) it does conform us to his suffering insofar as it is a work of love, a suffering undertaken for his Church in order to acquire her as his spouse."[8]

The sign of the sacrament of marriage is, therefore, a sign of redemption—of divine redemption which reaches to the bodies of men. And if it happens that this redemption is achieved by paths very different from those which human wisdom would seek out, we, as believers, should feel ourselves all the more secure because we can have greater confidence in God than in ourselves. So husband and wife, by freely accepting the sign of the grace of God in Christ, show that they are ready to remain faithful to each other throughout their life together—not in any manner but as God is faithful to his people, and as Christ is faithful, he who does not repent of the love he has shown us.[9]

───────────────

8. IV Sent., dist., 26, q. 2, a. 1, 3.

9. It is in view of the doctrine outlined here that Fr. Schillebeeckx could write as follows in the introduction to his little work on marriage as a sacrament: "The sacrament of marriage is a sign of love on the part of the heavenly Christ

The doctrine just outlined is reflected in the Second Vatican Council's 'vision' of marriage.[10] An intimate partnership of life and love, marriage was established by the Creator and is rooted in the irrevocable personal consent and covenant of the spouses. By their fully human and deeply personal act of mutual

who, in it, and in a real sense, draws close to the bridegroom and bride. The sacrament is Christ's gesture of love. In the sacramental sign of marriage his personal love for the couple as such becomes visible and perceptible. Just as at Cana, Christ is present at every marriage in order to do something and to say something. In an articulate and expressive gesture, he makes known to the newly-weds, and to all who are present at the ceremony, that it is he himself who joins together for life these two persons who already love each other with their whole heart. Of course, he had already brought them together at their first meeting and had helped them to grow to know each other, but on the day of their marriage he unites them more closely: he inspires in them a new and greater love like to that which he feels for his people, the Church. Hence the new spouses have only to let God act freely in them. They have only to say: "Yes, I do wish!" that is, I wish to let the work of God be accomplished in this sacred sign of our mutual commitment. That is why the consent of the husband and wife is first of all consent to the holy will of Christ. For it is because Christ wishes to give, each to the other, these two beings who love each other — in order that human love may free itself of earthly bonds and, even in its human aspect, become a sacred sign of greater and more profound love — that the partners must say "yes", without reserve, each to the other." Le Mariage est un Sacrament, p. 6.

10. **Pastoral Constitution on the Church in the Modern World**, Part II, Ch. I.

bestowal and acceptance, husband and wife set up an abiding relationship. And in their lives together they should become ever more aware of their communion, of their oneness.

Conjugal love has been blessed by Christ. For not only is Christian marriage structured on the model of Christ's union with his Church, but he enters into the lives of married Christians through the sacrament which he has given them. And he abides with them that their mutual love may grow. Caught up into the love of God and enriched by the redeeming grace of Christ, true married love not only leads the spouses to God but perfects their union and strengthens them in their office of father and mother.

Christian married love, merging the human with the divine, leads the spouses on to the mutual and full gift of themselves, a free gift proving itself by affection and in deed. Their love, which fills the whole of their lives, is expressed in a unique way and is perfected by the intimate giving of themselves in the marital act. This is an expression of mutual love, for marriage is not instituted only for procreation; it remains always a covenant relationship between two persons. So true is this that the essential value and the indissolubility of marriage remain intact in a childless marriage.

A concluding exhortation to Christian husbands

and wives strikingly presents the dignity and the challenge of the married state:

> Let the spouses themselves, made in the image of the living God and enjoying the authentic dignity of persons, be joined to one another in equal affection, harmony of mind, and the work of mutual sanctification. Thus they will follow Christ who is the principle of life. Thus, too, by the joys and sacrifices of their vocation and through their faithful love, married people will become witnesses of the mystery of that love which the Lord revealed to the world by his dying and his rising up to life again.[11]

11. Ibid., par. 52.